Eileen

To Gerald

January 1980.

from Iain

BURT'S LETTERS FROM THE
NORTH OF SCOTLAND.

BURT'S LETTERS

FROM

THE NORTH OF SCOTLAND.

With Facsimiles of the Original Engravings.

WITH AN INTRODUCTION

BY

R. JAMIESON, F.S.A.

AND THE HISTORY OF DONALD THE HAMMERER,

From an Authentic Account of the Family of Invernahyle; a MS. communicated by Sir WALTER SCOTT.

VOLUME SECOND.

JOHN DONALD PUBLISHERS LTD
EDINBURGH

First published in 1754 by
S. Birt, London.

Second Edition published in 1876
by William Paterson, Edinburgh.

Reprinted in 1974 by John Donald
Publishers Ltd., Edinburgh

ISBN 0 85976 002 2

Printed in Great Britain by
REDWOOD BURN LIMITED
Trowbridge & Esher

LETTERS

FROM

A Gentleman in the North of *Scotland*

TO

His FRIEND in *London* ;

CONTAINING

The Defcription of a Capital Town in that
Northern Country ;

WITH

An Account of fome uncommon Cuftoms
of the Inhabitants :

LIKEWISE

An Account of the HIGHLANDS, with the
Cuftoms and *Manners* of the HIGHLANDERS.

To which is added,

A LETTER relating to the MILITARY WAYS
among the Mountains, began in the Year 1726.

The Whole interfpers'd with *Facts* and *Circumftances*
intirely New to the Generality of People in *England*,
and little known in the Southern Parts of *Scotland*.

In TWO VOLUMES.

VOL. II.

LONDON:
Printed for S. BIRT, in *Ave-Maria-Lane*.

MDCCLIV.

CONTENTS OF VOL. II.

LETTER XIV.

LETTER XV.

LETTER XVI.

LETTER XVII.

LETTER XX.

LETTER XXIII.

LETTER XXIV.

LETTER XXV.

LETTER XXVI.

Concerning the New Roads, &c.

LETTER XIV.

IN my last Letter relating to this northern Part of the Low-Country, I promised (notwithstanding I should be engaged on the Subject of the Highlands) to give you an Account of any Thing else that should fall out by the Way, or recur to my Memory; But whether this Letter is to be placed to the High or Low-Country I leave you to determine, and I think it is not very material.

Some time ago a Highlander was executed here for Murder, and I am now about to give you some Account of his Education, Character, and Behaviour; and I flatter myself I shall do it at least as much to your Satisfaction as the Reverend Historiographer of Newgate.

You know I have rallied you several Times before now upon your bestowing, as I thought, too much Attention upon that Kind of Narrative, viz. the Session-Papers and last Dying Speeches.

This Man was by Trade a Smith, and dwelt near an English Foundry in Glengary, which lies between this Town and Fort William, of which Iron-Work I shall have some Occasion to speak more particularly before I conclude this Letter.

The Director of that Work had hired a Smith from England, and as it is said that Kings and Lovers can brook no Partners, so neither could the Highlander suffer the Rivalship of one of his own Trade, and therefore his Competitor was by him destined to die. One Night he came armed to the door of the Englishman's Hut with intent to kill him ; but the Man being for some Reason or other, apprehensive of Danger, had fastened the Door of his

Hovel more firmly than usual, and, while the Highlander was employed to force it open, he broke a Way through the back Wall of his House and made his Escape, but, being pursued, he cried out for Assistance; this brought a Lowland Scots Workman to endeavour to save him, and his generous Intention cost him his Life. Upon this several others took the Alarm and came up with the Murderer, whom they tried to secure; but he wounded some of them, and received several Wounds himself; however, he made his Escape for that Time. Three Days afterwards he was hunted out, and found among the Heath (which was then very high), where he had lain all that Time with his Wounds rankling, and without any Sustenance, not being able to get away because a continual Search was made all round about both Night and Day, and for the most Part within his Hearing; for it is more difficult to find a Highlander among the Heather, except newly tracked, than a Hare in her Form.

He was brought to this Town and committed to the *Tolbooth*, where Sentinels were posted to prevent his second Escape, which otherwise, in all Probability, would have been effected.

Some Time afterwards the Judges, in their Circuit, arrived here, and he was tried and condemned. Then the Ministers of the Town went to the Jail to give him their Ghostly Advice, and endeavoured to bring him to a Confession of his other Sins, without which they told him he could not hope for Redemption. For, besides this Murder, he was strongly suspected to have made away with his former Wife, with whose Sister he was known to have had too great a Familiarity. But when the Ministers had said all that is customary concerning the Merit of Confession, he abruptly asked them, if either or all of them could pardon him, in Case he made a Confession : and when they had answered—" No, not absolutely," he said, " You have told me, God can forgive me." They said it was true. " Then," said he, " as you cannot pardon me, I have nothing to do with you, but will confess to Him that can."

A little while after, a Smith of this Town was sent to take Measure of him, in order to make his Irons (for he was to be hanged in Chains), and, while the Man was doing it, the Highlander, with a Sneer, said—" Friend, you are now about to do a Job for a better Workman than yourself; I am certain I could fit you better than you can me."

When the Day for his Execution came (which by a late Law, could not be under Forty Days after his Condemnation), and I had resolved to stay at Home, though perhaps I should have been the only one in the Town that did so;—I say having taken that Resolution, a certain Lieutenant-Colonel, who is come into these Parts to visit his Friends, and is himself a Highlander, for whom I have the greatest Esteem; he came to me, and would have me bear him Company, declaring, at the same Time, that although he had a great

Desire to see how the Criminal would behave, yet he would wave all that, unless I would go with him; and, therefore, rather than disoblige my Friend, I consented, but I assure you with Reluctancy.

The Criminal was a little Fellow, but a fearless Desperado; and having annexed himself to the Clan of the Camerons, the Magistrates were apprehensive that some of the Tribe might attempt his Rescue; and therefore they made Application to the Commanding Officer for a whole Company of Men to guard him to the Place of Execution with greater Security.

Accordingly they marched him in the Centre, with two of the Ministers, one on each Side, talking to him by Turns all the Way for a Mile together. But I, not being accustomed to this Sort of Sights, could not forbear to reflect a little upon the Circumstance of a Man walking so far on Foot to his own Execution.

The Gibbet was not only erected upon the

Summit of a Hill, but was itself so high that it put me in mind of Haman's Gallows.

Being arrived at the Place, and the Ministers having done praying by him, the Executioner, a poor helpless Creature, of at least eighty Years of Age, ascended the Ladder. Then one of the Magistrates ordered the Malefactor to go up after him; upon which the Fellow turned himself hastily about; says he, " I did not think the Magistrates of Inverness had been such Fools, as to bid a Man go up a Ladder with his Hands tied behind him." And, indeed, I thought the great Burgher looked very silly, when he ordered the Fellow's Hands to be set at Liberty.

When the Knot was fixed, the old Hangman (being above the Criminal) began to feel about with his Feet to find some Footing whereby to come down beside the other, in order to turn him off, which I think could hardly have been done by a young Fellow the most nimble and alert, without getting under the Ladder, and coming down chiefly by his Hands.

Thus the Highlander, feeling the Executioner fumbling about him, in a little Time
seemed to lose all Patience; and turning himself about, with his Face from the Ladder, and
his Cap over his eyes, he cried out upon the
Trinity, which I daresay he had never heard
of before he was committed Prisoner for this
Fact, and then jumped off the Ladder. And
though his Hands were free, there did not
appear in them, or any other part of his Body,
the least Motion or Convulsion, any more
than if he had been a Statue.

It is true, I could not compare this with
other Things of the same Kind, but I thought
it a very bungling Execution, yet liked the
Cause of their Unskilfulness.

His Mother, who, it seems, is a very vile
Woman, and had bred him up in encouragement to Thieving and other Crimes, was
present, lying on the Heath at some little
Distance, when he leaped from the Ladder;
and at that Instant set up such a hideous
Shriek, followed by a screaming Irish Howl,

that every Body seemed greatly surprised at the uncommon Noise; and those who knew the Woman loaded her with Curses for being the Cause of this shameful End of her Son, who, they said, was naturally a Man of good Sense.

To conclude this Subject. The Smith who had made the Irons (I suppose frighted at the Execution) had run away, leaving his Tools behind him; and one of the Magistrates was forced to rivet them, there being none other that would undertake so shameful a Work for any Reward whatever.

But I had forgot to acquaint you that my Friend the Colonel, as we stood together all the while, favoured me with the Interpretation of that which passed, and most particularly what was said by the Criminal, who could not speak one Word of English.

You have now had a View of two tragic Scenes, viz. one at Glengary, and the other (being the Catastrophe) near Inverness;—at this Time a new Subject calls upon me to withdraw the latter Scene, and restore the former which represents Glengary.

Some few Years ago, a Company of Liverpool Merchants contracted with the Chieftain of this Tribe, at a great Advantage to him, for the Use of his Woods and other Conveniences for the Smelting of Iron ; and soon after, they put their Project in Execution, by building of Furnaces, sending Ore from Lancashire, &c.

By the Way, I should tell you that those Works were set up in this Country merely for the Sake of the Woods, because Iron cannot be made from the Ore with Sea or Pit Coal, to be malleable and fit for ordinary uses.

The Dwelling-House of this Chieftain had been burnt by the Troops in the Year 1715 ; but the Walls, which were of Stone, remained ; and therefore the Director of the above-mentioned Works thought it convenient to fit it up with new Timber, for the Use of himself or his Successors, during the Term of the Lease.

This being effectually done, a certain Number of Gentlemen of the Tribe came to him one Evening, on a seeming friendly Visit, whom he treated in a generous Manner, by giving them his best Wines and Provisions. Among other Things (though a Quaker by his religious Principles, yet is he a Man of polite Behaviour), he said to them something to this Purpose (for he told me himself how he had been used) : "Gentlemen, you have given me a great deal of Pleasure in this Visit ; and when you all, or any of you, will take the Trouble to repeat it, let it be when it will, you shall be welcome to any Thing that is in *my House*."

Upon those two last Words, one of them cried out—"G—d d—n you, sir ! your House? I thought it had been Glengary's House !" And upon those Watch-words they knocked out the Candles, fell upon him, wounded him, and got him down among them ; but he being strong and active, and the Darkness putting them in Confusion lest they should wound one another, he made a shift to slip from them in the Bustle, and to gain another Room. This he immediately barricaded, and cried out at the Window to his Workmen, that were not far off, who running to arm themselves and hasten to his Assistance, those *Gentlemen* made off.

It only now remains that I make some little Animadversion upon this rancorous, treacherous, and inhospitable Insult, which but for an Accident, it is much more than probable, would have gone by another Name.

Notwithstanding this House was repaired by Consent of the Chief, and, in Course of Time, he would have the Benefit of so great an expense, yet an English Trader dwelling in the *Castle*, as they call it, when at the same Time, the Laird inhabited a miserable Hut of Turf, as he did, and does to this Day;—this, I say, was intolerable to their Pride; and as it was apparently their design at first to raise a *Quarrelle d'Allemand* (a wrong-headed Quarrel), whatever other Words he had used, they would have found some among them that they might wrest to their inhuman Purpose. But those Words (*my House*) unluckily served in an eminent Degree to provoke their Rage, —as a Lunatic, who is reasonable by intervals, returns to his Ravings when any one touches upon the cause of his Madness. However, some Good arose from this Evil; for, upon Complaint made, the Chieftain was threatened with a great Number of Troops to be quartered upon him, and by that Means the Liverpool Company obtained some new advantageous Conditions to be added to their original Contract, which have made some Amends for the bad Usage of their Manager and Partner: and since that Time he has met with no ill Treatment from any of the Tribe, except some little Pilferings, which might have happened any where else.

I am next to give you a Conversation-Piece, which, with its Incidents, I foresee will be pretty spacious; but I shall make no Apology for it, because I know your leisure Hours to be as many as my own.

I have often heard it urged, as an undeniable Argument for the Truth of incredible Stories, that the Number and reputed Probity of the Witnesses to the Truth of a Fact is, or ought to be, sufficient to convince the most Incredulous. And I have known the Unbeliever to be treated by the greatest Part of a Company as an Infidel, or, at best, as a conceited Sceptic ; and that only because he could not, without a hypocritical Complaisance, own his Assent to the Truth of Relations the most repugnant to Reason and the well-known Laws and Operations of Nature.

The being accused of unreasonable Unbelief was, some Time ago, my own Circumstance ; and perhaps I have suffered in my Character, as a Christian (though Christianity has nothing to do with it), by disputing the Truth of a Tale, which I thought nobody above the ordinary Run of unthinking People could have believed—if upon Trust, without Examination, may be called Believing.

Upon making my first Visit to a certain

Lord not many Miles from this Town, I found there one of our Ministers of the Gospel; for so they called themselves, very probably for a Distinction between them and Ministers of State.

This Gentleman being in a declining Way in his Constitution, had been invited by our Lord (who I make no doubt has some particular View in making his Court to Presbyterian Clergy),—I say this Invitation to him was, to pass some Time in the Hills for the Benefit of the Mountain Air. But this was not a Compliment to him alone, but likewise to the whole Town ; for I do assure you none could be more esteemed than this Minister, for his affable Temper, exemplary Life, and what they call sound Doctrine. And for my own Part, I verily think, from some of what I am about to recite, that he was a *true Believer ;* for I do not in the least suspect him of Falsehood, it being so foreign to his known Character.

In the Evening, our noble Host, with the Minister and myself, sat down to a Bottle of

Champaign.　And after the Conversation had turned upon several Subjects, (I do not Remember how, but) Witchcraft was brought upon the Carpet.　By the Way, I did intend, after what I have formerly said upon that frivolous Subject, never to trouble you with it again.—But to my present Purpose.

After the Minister had said a good deal concerning the Wickedness of such a diabolical Practice as Sorcery ; and that I, in my Turn, had declared my Opinion of it which you knew many years ago ; he undertook to convince me of the reality of it by an Example, which is as follows :

A certain Highland Laird had found himself at several Times deprived of some Part of his Wine, and having so often examined his Servants about it, and none of them confessing, but all denying it with Asseverations, he was induced to conclude they were Innocent.

The next thing to consider was, how this could happen.　" Rats there were none to father the Theft.　Those, you know, according to your philosophical next-door Neighbour, might have drawn out the Corks with their Teeth, and then put in their Tails, which, being long and spungeous, would imbibe a good Quantity of Liquor. This they might suck out again, and so on, till they had emptied as many Bottles as were sufficient for their Numbers and the Strength of their Heads." But to be more serious :—I say, there was no Suspicion of Rats, and it was concluded it could be done by none but Witches.

Here the new Inquisition was set on Foot, and who they were was the Question ; but how should that be discovered ? To go the shortest Way to work, the Laird made Choice of one Night, and an Hour when he thought it might be watering-Time with the Hags ; and went to his Cellar without a Light, the better to surprise them. Then with his naked Broad-Sword in his Hand, he suddenly opened the Door, and shut it after him, and fell to cutting and slashing all round about him, till, at last, by an Opposition to the Edge of his

II.   B

Sword, he concluded he had at least wounded one of them. But I should have told you, that although the Place was very dark, yet he made no Doubt, by the Glare and Flashes of their Eyes that they were Cats ; but, upon the Appearance of a Candle, they were all vanished, and only some Blood left upon the Floor. I cannot forbear to hint in this Place at Don Quixotte's Battle with the *borachios* of Wine.

There was an old Woman, that lived about two Miles from the Laird's Habitation, reputed to be a Witch : her he greatly suspected to be one of the Confederacy, and immediately he hasted away to her Hut ; and, entering, he found her lying upon her Bed, and bleeding excessively.

This alone was some Confirmation of the Justness of his Suspicion; but casting his Eye under the Bed, there lay her Leg in its natural Form !

I must confess I was amazed at the Conclusion of this Narration : but ten Times more when, with the most serious Air, he assured me that he had seen a Certificate of the Truth of it, signed by four Ministers of that Part of the Country, and could procure me a Sight of it in a few Days, if I had the Curiosity to see it.

When he had finished his Story, I used all the Arguments I was Master of, to show him the Absurdity to suppose a Woman could be transformed into the Shape and diminutive Substance of a Cat; to vanish like a Flash of Fire; carry her Leg Home with her, &c. : and I told him, that if a Certificate of the Truth of it had been signed by every Member of the General Assembly, it would be impossible for me (however strong my Inclination were to believe) to bring my Mind to assent to it.   And at last I told him, that if it could be supposed to be true, it might be ranked in one's Imagination among the most Eminent Miracles.   Upon this last Word (like *my House* at Glengary) my good Lord, who had been silent all this while, said to the Minister— "Sir, you must not mind Mr——, for he is an Atheist."

I shall not remark upon the Politeness, good

Sense, and Hospitality of this Reflection; but this Imputation, although perhaps it might have passed with me for a Jest, or unheeded, before another, induced me, by my present Situation, to justify myself to the Kirk; and therefore it put me upon telling him, I was sorry his Lordship knew me no better, for that I thought there was nothing in the World, that is speculative, would admit of the thousandth Part of the Reasons for its Certainty, as would the Being of a Divine Providence; and that the visible Evidences were the stupendous Contrivance and Order of the Universe, the Fitness of all the Parts of every individual Creature for their respective Occasions, uses, and Necessities, &c.; and concluded, that none but an Idiot could imagine that senseless Atoms could jumble themselves into this wonderful Order and Economy. To this, and a good deal more to the same Purpose, our Host said nothing; perhaps he was conscious he had given his own Character for mine.

Then I turned to the Minister, and told him, that, for my own Part, I could not think there was any Thing irreligious in denying the supernatural Power of Witchcraft, because I had, early in my Youth, met with such Arguments as then convinced me, that the Woman of Endor was only an Impostor, like our Astrologers and Fortune-tellers, and not a Witch, in the present Acceptation of the Word; and, if my Memory did not deceive me, the principal Reasons were, that to support herself in her dishonest Profession, she must have been a Woman of Intelligence, and Intrigue, and therefore knew what passed in the World, and could not be ignorant of Saul's unhappy and abandoned State at that Time. Nor could she be unacquainted with the Person and Dress of the Prophet in his Lifetime, and therefore might easily describe him; and that Saul saw nothing, though he was in the same Room, but took it all from the Woman's Declaration.

Besides, I told him I might quote the Case

of Copernicus, who was not far from suffering Death for broaching his new System of the Earth, because it seemed to contradict a Text in the Psalms of David, although the same is now become unquestionable among the Astronomers, and is not at all disproved by the Divines. And to this I told him I might add an Inference relating to the present Belief of the Plurality of Habitable Worlds. Thus tenderly did I deal with a Man of his Modesty and ill State of Health.

I should have been ashamed to relate all this Egotism to any other than a truly Bosom-Friend, to whom one may and ought to talk as to one's self; for otherwise it is, by Distrust, to do him Injustice.

Some of these Ministers put me in Mind of Moliere's Physicians who were esteemed by the Faculty according as they adhered to, or neglected the Rules of Hippocrates and Galen ; and these, like them, will not go a Step out of the old Road, and therefore have not been accustomed to hear any Thing out of the ordinary Way, especially upon Subjects which, in their Notion, may have any Relation even to their traditional Tenets. And I think this close Adherency to Principles, in themselves indifferent, must be owing, in good Measure, to their Fear of the dreadful Word Heterodoxy. But this Gentleman heard all that I had to say against his Notion of Witchcraft with great Attention, either for the Novelty of it, or by Indulgence to a Stranger, or both. And I am fully persuaded it was the Newness of that Opposition which tempted him to sit up later than was convenient for him;—I say his sitting up only, because I think the very little he drank could make no Alteration in his Health; but not many Days after, I heard of his Death, which was much lamented by the People of this Town and the surrounding Country.

LETTER XV.

I HAVE hitherto been speaking only of the Part of Scotland where I am, viz. the eastern Side of this Island, bordering upon the northern Mountains, which Part I take to be a Kind of Medium between the Lowlands and Highlands, both by its Situation, and as it partakes of the Language and Customs of both those Extremes.

In England the Name of Scotsman is used indiscriminately to signify any one of the Male Part of the Natives of North Britain ; but the Highlanders differ from the People of the Low-Country in almost every Circumstance of Life. Their Language, Customs, Manners, Dress, &c., are unlike, and neither of them would be contented to be taken for the other, insomuch that in speaking of an unknown

Person of this Country (I mean Scotland) as a Scotsman only, it is as indefinite as barely to call a Frenchman an European, so little would his native Character be known by it.

I own it may be said there is a Difference in the other Part of this Island between the English and the Welsh ; but I think it is hardly in any Degree to be compared with the above-mentioned Distinction.

You will conclude I am speaking only of such among the People of Scotland who have not had the Advantages of Fortune and Education, for Letters and Converse with polite Strangers will render all Mankind equal, so far as their Genius and Application will admit ; some few Prejudices, of no very great Consequence, excepted.

A Crowd of other Remarks and Observations were just now pressing for Admittance, but I have rejected them all, as fit only to anticipate some of the Contents of the Sheets that are to follow ; and therefore I am now at Liberty to begin my Account of the most

northern Part of Great Britain, so far as it has
fallen within my Knowledge.

The Highlands take up more than one-half
of Scotland ; they extend from Dumbarton,
near the Mouth of the River Clyde, to the
northernmost Part of the Island, which is
above two-hundred Miles and their Breadth is
from fifty to above a Hundred ; but how to
describe them to you, so as to give you any
tolerable idea of such a rugged Country,—to
you, I say, who have never been out of the
South of England—is, I fear, a Task altogether
impracticable.

If it had been possible for me to procure a
Land-scape (I should say *Heath*-scape or *Rock*-
scape) of any one tremendous View among
the Mountains, it would be satisfactory and
informing at one single Cast of the Eye ; but
Language, you know, can only communicate Ideas, as it were, by Retail ; and a
Description of one Part of an Object, which
is composed of many, defaces or weakens
another that went before ; whereas Painting

not only shows the whole entire at one View, but leaves the several Parts to be examined separately and at Leisure by the Eye.

From Words we can only receive a Notion of such unknown Objects as bear some Resemblance with others we have seen, but Painting can even create Ideas of Bodies utterly unlike to any Thing that ever appeared to our Sight.

Thus am I entering upon my most difficult Task, for the Customs and Manners of the Highlanders will give me little Trouble more than the Transcribing; but as I believe I am the first who ever attempted a minute Description of any such Mountains I cannot but greatly doubt of my Success herein; and nothing but your Friendship and your Request (which to me is a Command) could have engaged me to hazard my Credit even with you, Indulgent as you are, by an Undertaking wherein the Odds are so much against me. But to begin.—The Highlands are, for the greatest Part, composed of Hills, as it were,

piled one upon another, till the Complication
rises and swells to Mountains, of which the
Heads are frequently above the Clouds, and
near the Summit have vast Hollows filled
up with Snow, which, on the North Side,
continues all the Year long.

From the west Coast they rise, as it were,
in Progression upwards, toward the Midland
Country Eastward (for on the East Side of the
Island they are not generally quite so high),
and their Ridges, for the most Part, run West
and East, or near those Points, as do likewise
all the yet discovered Beds or Seams of
Minerals they contain, with which, I have
good Reason to believe, they are well
furnished.

This Position of the Mountains has created
Arguments for the Truth of an universal
Deluge ; as if the Waters had formed those
vast Inequalities, by rushing violently from
East to West.

The Summits of the Highest are mostly
destitute of Earth ; and the huge naked Rocks,

being just above the Heath, produce the disagreeable Appearance of a scabbed Head,
especially when they appear to the View in a
conical Figure; for as you proceed round
them in Valleys, on lesser Hills, or the Sides
of other Mountains, their Form varies according to the Situation of the Eye that beholds
them.

They are clothed with Heath interspersed
with Rocks, and it is very rare to see any Spot
of Grass; for those (few as they are) lie
concealed from an outward View, in Flats and
Hollows among the Hills. There are, indeed,
some Mountains that have Woods of Fir, or
small Oaks on their Declivity, where the Root
of one Tree is almost upon a Line with the
Top of another: These are rarely seen in a
Journey; what there may be behind, out of
all common Ways, I do not know; but none
of them will pay for felling and removing over
Rocks, Bogs, Precipices, and Conveyance by
rocky Rivers, except such as are near the Sea-
Coast, and hardly those, as I believe the York

Buildings Company will find in the Conclusion.

I have already mentioned the Spaces of
Snow near the Tops of the Mountains: they
are great Hollows, appearing below as small
Spots of white (I will suppose of the Dimen-
sions of a pretty large Table), but they are so
diminished to the Eye by their vast Height
and Distance, from, perhaps, a Mile or more
in Length, and Breadth proportionable. This
I know by Experience, having ridden over such
a Patch of Snow in the Month of June: the
Surface was smooth, not slippery, and so hard
my Horse's Feet made little or no Impression
on it; and in one Place I rode over a Bridge
of Snow hollowed into a Kind of Arch. I
then made no doubt this Passage for the
Water, at Bottom of the deep Bourn, was
opened by the Warmth of Springs; of which,
I suppose, in dry Weather, the Current was
wholly composed.

From the Tops of the Mountains there
descend deep, wide, and winding Hollows,

ploughed into the Sides by the Weight and violent Rapidity of the Waters, which often loosen and bring down Stones of an incredible Bigness.

Of one of these Hollows, only Part appears to Sight in different Places of the Descent; the rest is lost to View in Meanders among the Hills.

When the uppermost Waters begin to appear with white Streaks in these Cavities, the Inhabitants who are within View of the Height say, *The Grey Mare's Tail begins to grow*, and it serves to them as a Monitor of ensuing Peril, if at that Time they venture far from Home; because they might be in Danger, by Waters, to have all Communication cut off between them and Shelter or Sustenance. And they are very skilful to judge in what Course of Time the Rivers and Bourns will become impassable.

The dashing and foaming of these Cataracts among the Rocks make them look exceedingly white, by Comparison with the bordering

Heath; but when the Mountains are covered
with Snow, and that is melting, then those
Streams of Water, compared with the white-
ness near them, look of a dirty yellowish
Colour, from the Soil and Sulphur mixed
with them as they descend. But every Thing,
you know, is this or that by Comparison.

I shall soon conclude this Description of
the outward Appearance of the Mountains
which I am already tired of, as a disagreeable
Subject, and I believe you are so too : but, for
your future Ease in that Particular, there is
not much Variety in it, but gloomy Spaces,
different Rocks, Heath, and high and low.

To cast one's Eye from an Eminence toward
a Group of them, they appear still one above
another, fainter and fainter, according to the
aerial Perspective, and the whole of a dismal
gloomy Brown drawing upon a dirty Purple ;
and most of all disagreeable when the Heath
is in Bloom.

Those Ridges of the Mountains that appear
next to the Ether—by their rugged irregular

Lines, the Heath and black Rocks—are rendered extremely harsh to the Eye, by appearing close to that diaphanous Body, without any Medium to soften the Opposition; and the clearer the Day, the more rude and offensive they are to the Sight; yet, in some few Places, where any white Crags are a-top, that Harshness is something softened.

But of all the Views, I think the most horrid is, to look at the Hills from East to West, or *vice versâ*, for then the Eye penetrates far among them, and sees more particularly their stupendous Bulk, frightful Irregularity, and horrid Gloom, made yet more *sombrous* by the Shades and faint Reflections they communicate one to another.

As a Specimen of the Height of those Mountains, I shall here take notice of one in Lochaber, called Ben-Nevis, which, from the Level below to that Part of the Summit only which appears to View, has been several times measured by different Artists, and found to

II. C

be three-Quarters of a Mile of perpendicular Height.

It is reckoned seven Scots Miles to that Part where it begins to be inaccessible.

Some English Officers took it in their Fancy to go to the Top, but could not attain it for Bogs and huge perpendicular Rocks; and when they were got as high as they could go, they found a vast Change in the Quality of the Air, saw nothing but the Tops of other Mountains, and altogether a Prospect of one tremendous Heath, with here and there some Spots of Crags and Snow.

This wild Expedition, in ascending round and round the Hills, in finding accessible Places, helping one another up the Rocks, in Disappointments, and their returning to the Foot of the Mountain, took them up a whole Summer's Day, from five in the Morning. This is according to their own Relation. But they were fortunate in an Article of the greatest Importance to them, *i.e.* that the Mountain happened to be free from Clouds while they were in it, which is a Thing not very common in that dabbled Part of the Island, the Western Hills ;—I say, if those condensed Vapours had passed while they were at any considerable Height, and had continued, there would have been no Means left for them to find their Way down, and they must have perished with Cold, Wet, and Hunger.

In passing to the Heart of the Highlands we proceeded from bad to worse, which makes the *worst of all* the less surprising : but I have often heard it said by my Countrymen, that they verily believed, if an Inhabitant of the South of England were to be brought blindfold into some narrow, rocky Hollow, enclosed with these horrid prospects, and there to have his Bandage taken off, he would be ready to die with Fear, as thinking it impossible he should ever get out to return to his Native Country.

Now what do you think of a poetical Mountain, smooth and easy of Ascent, clothed with a verdant, flowery Turf, where Shepherds tend their Flocks, sitting under the

Shade of small Poplars, &c?—In short, what do you think of Richmond Hill, where we have passed so many Hours together, delighted with the beautiful prospect.

But after this Description of these Mountains, it is not unlikely you may ask, of what Use can be such monstrous Excrescences?

To this I should answer, they contain Minerals, as I said before; and serve for the breeding and feeding of Cattle, wild Fowls, and other useful Animals, which cost little or nothing in keeping. They break the Clouds, and not only replenish the Rivers, but collect great Quantities of Water into Lakes and other vast Reservoirs, where they are husbanded, as I may say, for the Use of Mankind in Time of Drought; and thence, by their Gravity, perforate the Crannies of Rocks and looser Strata, and work their Way either perpendicularly, horizontally, or obliquely; the two latter, when they meet with solid Rock, Clay, or some other resisting Stratum, till they find their proper Passages downward,

and in the End form the Springs below.   And,
certainly, it is the Deformity of the Hills that
makes the Natives conceive of their naked
Straths and *Glens*, as of the most beautiful
Objects in Nature.

But as I suppose you are Unacquainted
with these Words, I shall here take Occasion
to explain them to you.

A *Strath* is a flat Space of arable Land,
lying along the Side or Sides of some capital
River, between the Water and the Feet of the
Hills ; and keeps its Name till the River comes
to be confined to a narrow Space, by stony
Moors, Rocks, or Windings among the
Mountains.

The *Glen* is a little Spot of Corn Country,
by the Sides of some small River or Rivulet,
likewise bounded by Hills ; this is in general :
but there are some Spaces that are called
Glens, from there being Flats in deep Hollows
between the high Mountains, although they
are perfectly barren, as *Glen-dou* (or the black
glen), Glen-Almond, &c.

By the Way, this Glen-Almond is a Hollow so very narrow, and the Mountains on each Side so steep and high, that the Sun is seen therein no more than between two and three Hours in the longest Day.

Now let us go among the Hills, and see if we can find something more agreeable than their outward Appearance. And to that End I shall give you the Journal of two Days' Progress; which, I believe, will better answer the Purpose than a disjointed Account of the Inconveniences, Hazards, and Hardships, that attend a Traveller in the Heart of the Highlands. But before I begin the particular Account of my Progress, I shall venture at a general Description of one of the Mountain Spaces, between Glen and Glen: and when that is done, you may make the Comparison with one of our southern Rambles; in which, without any previous *route*, we used to wander from Place to Place, just so as the Beauty of the Country invited.

How have we been pleased with the easy

Ascent of an Eminence, which almost imperceptibly brought us to the beautiful Prospects seen from its summit! What a delightful Variety of Fields, and Meadows of various Tints of Green, adorned with Trees and blooming Hedges ; and the whole embellished with Woods, Groves, Waters, Flocks, Herds, and magnificent Seats of the Happy (at least seemingly so); and every other rising Ground opening a new and lovely Landscape !

But in one of these *Monts* (as the Highlanders call them), soon after your Entrance upon the first Hill, you lose, for good and all, the Sight of the Plain from whence you parted ; and nothing follows but the View of Rocks and Heath, both beneath and on every Side, with high and barren Mountains round about.

Thus you creep slowly on, between the Hills in rocky Ways, sometimes over those Eminences, and often on their Declivities, continually hoping the next Ridge before you will be the Summit of the highest, and so often deceived in that Hope, as almost to despair of ever reaching the Top. And thus you are still rising by long Ascents, and again descending by shorter, till you arrive at the highest Ground; from whence you go down in much the same Manner, reversed, and never have the Glen in View that you wish to see, as the End of your present Trouble, till you are just upon it. And when you are there, the Inconveniences (though not the Hazards) are almost as great as in the tedious Passage to it.

As an Introduction to my Journal, I must acquaint you that I was advised to take with me some cold Provisions, and Oats for my Horses, there being no Place of Refreshment till the End of my first Day's Journey.

The 2d of *October*, 172—

Set out with one Servant and a Guide; the latter, because no Stranger (or even a Native, unacquainted with the Way) can venture among the Hills without a Con-

ductor; for if he once go aside, and most
especially if Snow should fall (which may
happen on the very high Hills at any Season
of the Year), in that, or any other Case, he
may wander into a Bog to impassable Bourns
or Rocks, and every *ne plus ultra* oblige him
to change his Course, till he wanders from all
Hopes of ever again seeing the Face of a human Creature. Or if he should accidentally
hit upon the Way from whence he strayed, he
would not distinguish it from another, there is
such a seeming Sameness in all the rocky
Places. Or again, if he should happen to
meet with some Highlander, and one that was
not unwilling to give him Directions, he could
not declare his Wants, as being a Stranger to
the Language of the Country. In short, one
might as well think of making a Sea Voyage
without Sun, Moon, Stars, or Compass, as
pretend to know which way to take, when
lost among the Hills and Mountains.

But to return to my Journal from which I
have strayed, though not with much Danger,

it being at first setting out, and my Guide with
me.

After riding about four Miles of pretty good
Road over heathy Moors, hilly, but none high
or of steep Ascent, I came to a small River,
where there was a Ferry; for the Water was
too deep and rapid to pass the Ford above.
The Boat was patched almost every where with
rough Pieces of Boards, and the Oars were kept
in their Places by small Bands of twisted Sticks.

I could not but inquire its Age, seeing it
had so many Marks of Antiquity; and was
told by the Ferryman it had belonged to his
Father, and was above sixty Years old. This
put me in mind of the Knife, which was of an
extraordinary Age, but had, at Times, been
repaired with many new Blades and Handles.
But in most Places of the Highlands, where
there is a Boat (which is very rare), it is much
worse than this, and not large enough to receive a Horse; and therefore he is swum at
the Stern, while somebody holds up his Head
by a Halter or Bridle.

The Horses swim very well at first setting out; but if the Water be wide, in Time they generally turn themselves on one of their Sides, and patiently suffer themselves to be dragged along.

I remember one of these Boats was so very much out of Repair, we were forced to stand upon Clods of Turf to stop the Leaks in her Bottom, while we passed across the River.

I shall here conclude, in the Style of the News-Writers——This to be continued in my next.

LETTER XVI.

FROM the River's Side I ascended a steep Hill, so full of large Stones, it was impossible to make a Trot. This continued up and down about a Mile and Half.

At the Foot of the Hill, tolerable Way for a Mile, there being no great Quantity of Stones among the Heath, but very uneven; and, at the End of it, a small Bourn descending from between two Hills, worn deep among the Rocks, rough, rapid, and steep, and dangerous to pass. I concluded some Rain had fallen behind the Hills that were near me; which I could not see, because it had a much greater Fall of Water than any of the like Kind I had passed before.

From hence a Hill five Miles over, chiefly composed of lesser Hills; so stony, that it was impossible to crawl above a Mile in an Hour.

But I must except a small Part of it from this general Description; for there ran across this Way (or *Road*, as they call it) the End of a Wood of Fir-Trees, the only one I had ever passed.

This, for the most Part, was an easy, rising Slope of about half a Mile. In most Places of the Surface it was Bog about two Feet deep, and beneath was uneven Rock; in other Parts the Rock and Roots of the Trees appeared to View.

The Roots sometimes crossed one another, as they ran along a good Way upon the Face of the Rock, and often above the boggy Part, by both which my Horses' Legs were so much entangled, that I thought it impossible to keep them upon their Feet. But you would not have been displeased to observe how the Roots had run along, and felt, as it were, for the Crannies of the Rock; and there shot into them, as a Hold against the Pressure of Winds above.

At the End of this Hill was a River, or

rather Rivulet, and near the Edge of it a small grassy Spot, such as I had not seen in all my Way, but the Place not inhabited. Here I stopped to bait. My own Provisions were laid upon the Foot of a Rock, and the Oats upon a Kind of mossy Grass, as the cleanest Place for the Horses' feeding.

While I was taking some Refreshment, Chance provided me with a more agreeable Repast—the Pleasure of the Mind. I happened to espy a poor Highlander at a great Height, upon the Declivity of a high Hill, and ordered my Guide to call him down. The *trout so* (or come hither) seemed agreeable to him, and he came down with wonderful Celerity, considering the Roughness of the Hill; and asking what was *my Will* (in his Language), he was given to understand I wanted him only to eat and drink. This unexpected Answer raised such Joy in the poor Creature, that he could not help showing it by skipping about, and expressing Sounds of Satisfaction. And when I was retired a little

Way down the River, to give the Men an Opportunity of enjoying themselves with less Restraint, there was such Mirth among the Three, as I thought a sufficient Recompense for my former Fatigue.

But, perhaps, you may question how there could be such Merriment, with nothing but water?

I carried with me a Quart-Bottle of Brandy, for my Man and the Guide; and for myself, I had always in my Journeys a *Pocket-Pistol*, loaded with Brandy, mixed with Juice of Lemon (when they were to be had), which again mingled with Water in a wooden Cup, was, upon such Occasions, my Table-Drink.

When we had trussed up our Baggage, I entered the Ford, and passed it not without Danger, the Bottom being filled with large Stones, the Current rapid, a steep, rocky Descent to the Water, and a Rising on the further Side much worse; for having mounted a little Way up the Declivity, in turning the Corner of a Rock I came to an exceedingly

steep Part before I was aware of it, where I
thought my Horse would have gone down
backwards, much faster than he went up; but
I recovered a small Flat of the Rock, and dis-
mounted.

There was nothing remarkable afterwards,
till I came near the Top of the Hill; where
there was a seeming Plain, of about a hundred
and fifty Yards, between me and the Summit.

No sooner was I upon the Edge of it, but
my Guide desired me to alight; and then I
perceived it was a Bog, or Peat-moss, as they
call it.

I had Experience enough of these deceitful
Surfaces to order that the Horses should be led
in separate Parts, lest, if one broke the Turf,
the other, treading in his Steps, might sink.

The Horse I used to ride, having little
Weight but his own, went on pretty success-
fully; only now and then breaking the Surface
a little; but the other, that carried my Portmanteau, and being not quite so nimble, was
much in Danger, till near the further End, and

there he sank. But it luckily happened to be in a Part where his long Legs went to the Bottom, which is generally hard Gravel, or Rock; but he was in almost up to the Back.

By this Time my own (for Distinction) was quite free of the Bog, and being frighted, stood very tamely by himself; which he would not have done at another Time. In the meanwhile we were forced to wait at a Distance, while the other was flouncing and throwing the Dirt about him; for there was no Means of coming near him to ease him of the heavy Burden he had upon his Loins, by which he was sometimes in danger to be turned upon his Back, when he rose to break the Bog before him. But, in about a Quarter of an Hour, he got out, bedaubed with the Slough, shaking with Fear, and his Head and Neck all over in a Foam.

This Bog was stiff enough at that Time to bear the Country *Garrons* in any Part of it. But it is observed of the English Horses, that when they find themselves hampered, they

II   D

stand still, and tremble till they sink, and then they struggle violently, and work themselves further in; and if the Bog be deep, as most of them are, it is next to impossible to get them out, otherwise than by digging them a Passage. But the little Highland Hobbies, when they find themselves bogged, will lie still till they are relieved. And besides, being bred in the Mountains, they have learnt to avoid the weaker Parts of the Mire; and sometimes our own Horses, having put down their Heads and smelt to the Bog, will refuse to enter upon it.

There is a certain Lord in one of the most northern Parts, who makes Use of the little *Garrons* for the Bogs and rough Ways, but has a sizeable Horse led with him, to carry him through the deep and rapid Fords.

As for myself, I was harassed on this Slough, by winding about from Place to Place, to find such Tufts as were within my Stride or Leap, in my heavy Boots with high Heels; which, by my Spring, when the little Hillocks were too far asunder, broke the Turf, and

then I threw myself down toward the next
Protuberance : but to my Guide it seemed
nothing ; he was light of Body, shod with
flat *Brogues*, wide in the Soles, and accustomed to a particular Step, suited to the
Occasion.

This Hill was about three Quarters of a
Mile over, and had but a short Descent on
the Further Side, rough, indeed, but not
remarkable in this Country.   I had now five
computed Miles to go before I came to my
first Asylum,—that is, five Scots Miles, which,
as in the North of England, are longer than
yours as three is to two ; and, if the Difficulty
of the Way were to be taken into Account, it
might well be called Fifteen.   This, except
about three Quarters of a Mile of heathy
Ground, pretty free from Stones and Rocks,
consisted of stony Moors, almost impracticable
for a Horse with his Rider, and likewise of
rocky Way, where we were obliged to dis-
mount, and sometimes climb, and otherwhile
slide down.   But what vexed me most of all,

they called it a Road ; and yet I must confess it was preferable to a boggy Way. The great Difficulty was to wind about with the Horses, and find such Places as they could possibly be got over.

When we came near the Foot of the Lowermost Hill, I discovered a pretty large Glen, which before was not to be seen. I believe it might be about a Quarter of a Mile wide, enclosed by exceedingly high Mountains, with nine dwelling-Huts, besides a few others of a lesser Size for Barns and Stables : this they call a Town with a pompous Name belonging to it ; but the Comfort of being near the End of my Day's Journey, heartily tired, was mixed with the Allay of a pretty River, that ran between me and my Lodging.

Having passed the Hill, I entered the River, my Horse being almost at once up to his Midsides ; the Guide led him by the Bridle, as he was sometimes climbing over the loose Stones which lay in all Positions, and many of them two or three Feet diameter ; at other Times

with his Nose in the Water and mounted up
behind. Thus he proceeded with the utmost
Caution, never removing one Foot till he found
the others firm, and all the while seeming
impatient of the Pressure of the Torrent, as if
he was sensible that, once losing his Footing,
he should be driven away and dashed against
the Rocks below.

In other rapid Rivers, where I was something acquainted with the Fords, by having
passed them before, though never so Stony, I
thought the leader of my Horse to be an Incumbrance to him ; and I have always found,
as the Rivers while they are passable, are
pretty clear, the Horse is the surest Judge of
his own Safety. Perhaps some would think
it strange I speak in this Manner of a
Creature that we proudly call irrational.
There is a certain Giddiness attends the
violent Passage of the Water when one is in
it, and therefore I always, at entering, resolved
to keep my Eye steadily fixed on some
remarkable Stone on the Shore of the further

Side, and my Horse's Ears, as near as I could, in a Line with it, leaving him to choose his Steps; for the Rider, especially if he casts his Eye down the Torrent, does not know whether he goes directly forward or not, but fancies he is carried, like the Leeway of a Ship, Sideways along with the Stream. If he cannot forbear looking aside, it is best to turn his Face toward the coming Current.

Another Precaution is (and you cannot use too many), to let your Legs hang in the Water; and, where the Stones will permit, to preserve a firmer Seat, in case of any sudden Slide or Stumble.

By what I have been saying you will perceive I still retain the Custom of my own Country, in not sending my Servant before me through these dangerous Waters, as is the constant Practice of all the Natives of Scotland; nor could I prevail with myself to do so, at least unless, like theirs, mine went before me in smooth as well as bad Roads. But in that there are several Inconveniences: and although a Servant may by some be contemned for his servile Circumstance of Life, I could never bear the Thoughts of Exposing him to Dangers for my own Safety and Security, lest he should despise me with more Justice, and in a greater Degree, for the Want of a necessary Resolution and Fortitude.

I shall here mention a whimsical Expedient against the Danger of these Highland Fords.

An Officer who was lately quartered at one of the Barracks in a very mountainous Part of the Country, when he travelled, carried with him a long Rope ; this was to be put round his Body, under his Arms, and those that attended him were to wade the River, and hold the Rope on the other Side, that, if any Accident should happen to him by Depth of Water, or the Failure of his Horse, they might prevent his being carried down the Current and drag him ashore.

The Instant I had recovered the further Side of the River, there appeared, near the Water, six Highland Men and a Woman; these,

I suppose had coasted the Stream over Rocks, and along the Sides of steep Hills, for I had not seen them before. Seeing they were preparing to wade, I staid to observe them : first the Men and the Woman tucked up their Petticoats, then they cast themselves into a Rank, with the Female in the Middle, and laid their Arms over one another's Shoulders; and I saw they had placed the strongest toward the Stream, as best able to resist the Force of the Torrent. In their Passage, the large Slippery Stones, made some of them now and then lose their Footing: and, on those Occasions, the whole Rank changed Colour and Countenance.

I believe no Painter ever remarked such strong Impressions of Fear and Hope on a human Face, with so many and sudden Successions of those two opposite Passions, as I observed among those poor People; but in the Highlands this is no uncommon Thing.

Perhaps you will ask—" How does a single Highlander support himself against so great a Force?" He bears himself up against the

Stream with a Stick, which he always carries with him for that Purpose.

As I am now at the End of my first Day's Journey, and have no Mind to resume this disagreeable Subject in another Place, I shall ask leave to mention one Danger more attending the Highland Fords; and that is, the sudden Gushes of Waters that sometimes descend from behind the adjacent Hills, insomuch that, when the River has not been above a Foot Deep, the Passenger, thinking himself secure, has been overtaken and carried away by the Torrent.

Such Accidents have happened twice within my Knowledge, in two different small Rivers, both within seven Miles of this Town; one to an Exciseman and the Messenger who was carrying him from hence to Edinburgh, in order to answer some Accusations relating to his Office; the other to two young Fellows of a neighbouring Clan;—all drowned in the Manner above-mentioned. And, from these two Instances, we may reasonably conclude that many Accidents of the same Nature have happened, especially in more Mountainous Parts, and those hardly ever known but in the narrow Neighbourhoods of the unhappy Sufferers.

When I came to my *Inn*, I found the Stable Door too low to receive my large Horses, though high enough for the Country Garrons ; so the Frame was taken out, and a small Part of the Roof pulled down for their Admittance ; for which Damage I had a Shilling to pay the next Morning. My Fear was, the Hut being weak and small, they would pull it about their Ears ; for that Mischance had happened to a Gentleman who bore me Company in a former Journey, but his Horses were not much hurt by the Ruins.

When Oats were brought I found them so light and so much sprouted, that taking up a handful, others hung to them, in Succession, like a Cluster of Bees ; but of such Corn it is the Custom to give double Measure.

My next Care was to provide for myself, and

to that End I entered the dwelling-House.
There my Landlady sat, with a Parcel of
Children about her, some quite, and others
almost, naked, by a little Peat Fire, in the
Middle of the Hut ; and over the Fire-Place
was a small Hole in the Roof for a Chimney.
The Floor was common Earth, very uneven, and
no where Dry, but near the Fire and in the
Corners, where no Foot had carried the
muddy Dirt from without Doors.

The Skeleton of the Hut was formed of
small crooked Timber, but the Beam for the
Roof was large out of all Proportion. This is
to render the Weight of the whole more fit to
resist the violent Flurries of Wind that frequently rush into the Plains from the Openings
of the Mountains ; for the whole Fabric was
set upon the Surface of the Ground like a
Table, Stool or other Moveable.

Hence comes the Highlander's Compliment,
or Health, in drinking to his Friend ; for as we
say, among Familiar Acquaintance, " To your
Fire-Side ; " he says, much to the same Pur-

pose, " To your *Roof-Tree*," alluding to the Family's Safety from Tempests.

The Walls were about four Feet high, lined with Sticks wattled like a Hurdle, built on the Outside with Turf; and thinner Slices of the same serve for Tiling. This last they call *Divet*.

When the Hut has been Built some Time it is covered with Weeds and Grass; and, I do assure you, I have seen Sheep, that had got up from the Foot of an adjoining Hill feeding upon the Top of the House.

If there happened to be any Continuance of dry Weather, which is pretty rare, the Worms drop out of the *Divet* for want of Moisture, insomuch that I have shuddered at the Apprehension of their falling into the Dish when I have been eating.

LETTER XVII.

AT a little Distance was another Hut,
where Preparations where making for
my Reception. It was something less but
contained two Beds, or Boxes to lie in,
and was kept as an Apartment for People
of Distinction;—or, which is all one, for
such as seem by their Appearance to
promise Expense. And, indeed, I have
often found but little Difference in that
Article, between one of those Huts and
the best Inn in England. Nay if I were to
reckon the Value of what I had for my own
Use by the Country Price, it would appear to
be Ten Times dearer: but it is not the
Maxim of the Highlands alone (as we know),
that those who travel must pay for such as
stay at Home; and really the Highland
Gentlemen themselves are less scrupulous of

Expense in these public Huts than anywhere else. And their Example, in great Measure, authorises Impositions upon Strangers, who may complain, but can have no redress.

The Landlord not only sits down with you, as in the northern Lowlands, but, in some little Time, asks leave and sometimes not, to introduce his Brother, Cousin, or more, who are all to drink your Honour's Health in Usky; which, though a strong Spirit, is to them like Water. And this I have often seen them drink out of a Scallop-Shell. And in other Journeys, notwithstanding their great Familiarity with me, I have several Times seen my Servant at a Loss how to behave, when the Highlander has turned about and very formally drank to him : and when I have baited, and eaten two or three Eggs, and nothing else to be had, when I asked the question, " What is there for eating ? " the Answer has been, " Nothing for you, sir ; but Six-pence for your Man."

The Host, who is rarely other than a Gentleman, is Interpreter between you and those who do not speak English ; so that you lose nothing of what any one has to say relating to the Antiquity of their Family, or the heroic Actions of their Ancestors in War with some other Clan.

If the Guest be a Stranger, not seen before by the Man of the House, he takes the first Opportunity to inquire of the Servant from whence his Master came, who he is, whither he is going, and what his Business in that Country? And if the Fellow happens to be surly as thinking the Inquiry impertinent, perhaps chiefly from the Highlander's poor Appearance, then the Master is sure to be subtilly sifted (if not asked) for the Secret ; and, if obtained, it is a Help to Conversation with his future Guests.

Notice at last was brought me that my Apartment was ready ; but at going out from the first Hovel, the other seemed to be all on Fire within : for the Smoke came pouring out through the Ribs and Roof all over; but chiefly out at the Door, which was not four Feet high, so that the whole made the Appearance (I have seen) of a fuming Dunghill removed and fresh piled up again, and pretty near the same in Colour, Shape, and Size.

By the Way the Highlanders say they love the Smoke; it keeps them warm. But I retired to my first Shelter till the Peats were grown red, and the Smoke thereby abated.

This Fuel is seldom kept dry, for want of Convenience; and that is one Reason why, in Lighting or replenishing the Fire, the Smokiness continues so long a Time;—and Moggy's puffing of it with her Petticoat, instead of a Pair of Bellows, is a dilatory Way.

I believe you would willing know (being an Englishman) what I had to Eat. My Fare was a Couple of roasted Hens (as they call them), very poor, new killed, the Skins much broken with plucking; black with Smoke, and greased with bad Butter.

As I had no great Appetite to that Dish, I spoke for some hard Eggs; made my Supper of the Yolks, and washed them down with a Bottle of good small Claret.

My Bed had clean Sheets and Blankets! but, which was best of all (though Negative), I found no Inconvenience from those troublesome Companions with which most other Huts abound. But the bare Mention of them brings to my Remembrance a Passage between two Officers of the Army, the Morning after a Highland Night's Lodging. One was taking off the slowest kind of the two, when the other cried out, "Z——ds! what are you doing?—Let us first secure the Dragoons; we can take the Foot at Leisure."

But I had like to have forgot a Mischance that happened to me the next Morning; for rising early, and getting out of my Box pretty hastily, I unluckily set my Foot in the Chamber-Pot, a Hole in the Ground by the Bed-side, which was made to serve for that Use in case of Occasion.

I shall not trouble you with any Thing that passed till I mounted on Horseback; only, for

II. E

want of something more proper for Breakfast, I took up with a little Brandy, Water, Sugar, and Yolks of Eggs, beat up together; which I think they call Old Man's Milk.

I was now provided with a new Guide, for the Skill of my first extended no further than this place: but this could speak no English, which I found afterwards to be an Inconvenience.

Second Day.—At mounting I received many Compliments from my Host; but the most earnest was, that common one of wishing me Good Weather. For, like the Seafaring-Man, my Safety depended upon it; especially at that Season of the Year.

As the Plain lay before me, I thought it all fit for Culture; but in riding along, I observed a good deal of it was Bog, and here and there Rock even with the Surface: however, my Road was smooth; and if I had had Company with me, I might have said jestingly, as was usual among us after a rough Way, "Come, let us ride this over again."

At the End of about a Mile, there was a
steep Ascent, which they call a *Carne*;—that
is, an exceedingly stony Hill, which at some
Distance seems to have no Space at all between
Stone and Stone. I thought I could compare
it with no Ruggedness so aptly as to suppose it
like all the different Stones in a Mason's Yard
thrown promiscuously upon one another.
This I passed on foot, at the Rate of about half
a Mile in the Hour. I do not reckon the Time
that was lost in backing my Horses out of a
narrow Place without-side of a Rock, where the
Way ended with a Precipice of about twenty
Feet deep. Into this Gap they were led by the
Mistake or Carelessness of my Guide. The
Descent from the Top of this Carne was
short, and thence I ascended another Hill not
so stony ; and at last, by several others (which,
though very rough, are not reckoned extraordinary in the Highlands), I came to a
Precipice of about a hundred Yards in
Length.

The Side of the Mountain below me was

almost perpendicular; and the rest above, which seemed to reach the Clouds, was exceedingly steep. The Path which the Highlanders and their little Horses had worn was scarcely two Feet wide, but pretty smooth; and below was a Lake whereinto vast Pieces of Rock had fallen, which I suppose had made, in some Measure, the Steepness of the Precipice; and the Water that appeared between some of them seemed to be under my Stirrup. I really believe the Path where I was is twice as high from the Lake as the Cross of St. Paul's is from Ludgate-Hill; and I thought I had good Reason to think so, because a few Huts beneath, on the further Side of the Water, which is not very wide, appeared to me each of them like a black Spot not much bigger than the Standish before me.

A certain Officer of the Army going this Way was so terrified with the Sight of the Abyss that he crept a little higher, fondly imagining he should be safer above, as being further off from the Danger, and so to take

hold of the Heath in his Passage. There a
panic Terror seized him, and he began to lose
his Forces, finding it impracticable to proceed,
and being fearful to quit his Hold and slide
down, lest in so doing he should overshoot the
narrow Path; and had not two Soldiers come
to his Assistance, viz. one who was at some
little Distance before him, and the other
behind, in all Probability he had gone to the
Bottom. But I have observed that particular
Minds are wrought upon by particular
Dangers, according to their different sets of
Ideas. I have sometimes travelled in the
Mountains with Officers of the Army, and
have known one in the Middle of a deep and
rapid Ford cry out he was undone; another
was terrified with the Fear of his Horse's
falling in an exceeding Rocky Way; and perhaps neither of them would be so much
shocked at the Danger that so greatly affected
the other; or, it may be, either of them at
standing the Fire of a Battery of Cannon.
But for my own Part I had passed over two

such Precipices before, which rendered it something less terrifying; yet, as I have hinted, I
chose to ride it, as I did the last of the other
two, knowing by the first I was liable to Fear,
and that my Horse was not subject either to
that disarming Passion or to Giddiness, which
in that Case I take to be the Effect of
Apprehension.

It is a common Thing for the Natives to
ride their Horses over such little Precipices;
but for myself I never was upon the Back of
one of them; and, by the Account some
Highlanders have given me of them, I think I
should never choose it in such Places as I have
been describing.

There is in some of those Paths, at the
very Edge, or Extremity, a little mossy Grass,
and those *Sheltys*, being never shod, if they
are ever so little Foot-sore, they will, to favour
their Feet, creep to the very Brink, which
must certainly be very terrible to a Stranger.

It will hardly ever be out of my Memory, how
I was haunted by a kind of poetical Sentence,

after I was over this Precipice, which did not cease till it was supplanted by the new Fear of my Horse's falling among the Rocks in my Way from it.   It was this :—

"There hov'ring Eagles wait the fatal Trip."

By the Way, this Bird is frequently seen among the Mountains, and, I may say, severely felt sometimes, by the Inhabitants, in the loss of their Lambs, Kids, and even Calves and Colts.

I had now gone about six Miles, and had not above two, as I understood afterwards, to the Place of baiting.   In my Way, which I shall only say was very rough and hilly, I met a Highland Chieftain with fourteen Attendants, whose Offices about his Person I shall hereafter describe, at least the greatest Part of them.   When we came, as the Sailor says, almost Broadside and Broadside, he eyed me as if he would look my Hat off; but, as he was at Home, and I a Stranger in the Country, I thought he might have made the first

Overture of Civility, and therefore I took little Notice of him and his ragged Followers. On his Part he seemed to show a Kind of Disdain at my being so slenderly attended, with a Mixture of Anger that I showed him no Respect before his Vassals ; but this might only be my Surmise—yet it looked very like it. I supposed he was going to the Glen from whence I came, for there was no other Hut in all my Way, and there he might be satisfied by the Landlord who I was, &c.

I shall not trouble you with any more at present, than that I safely arrived at my baiting Place ; for, as I hinted before, there is such a Sameness in the Parts of the Hills that the Description of one rugged Way, Bog, Ford, &c., will serve pretty well to give you a Notion of the rest.

Here I desired to know what I could have for Dinner, and was told there was some undressed Mutton. This I esteemed as a Rarity, but, as I did not approve the Fingers of either Maid or Mistress, I ordered my Man (who is an excellent Cook, so far as a Beef-Steak or a Mutton-chop) to broil me a Chop or two, while I took a little Turn to ease my Legs, weary with sitting so long on Horseback.

This proved an intolerable Affront to my Landlady, who raved and stormed, and said, " What's your Master? I have dressed for the Laird of this and the Laird of that, such and such Chiefs; and this very Day," says she, " for the Laird of ——," who, I doubted not, was the Person I met on the Hill. To be short, she absolutely refused to admit of any such Innovation; and so the Chops served for my man and the Guide, and I had Recourse to my Former Fare hard Eggs.

Eggs are seldom wanting at the public Huts, though, by the Poverty of the Poultry, one might wonder how they should have any Inclination to produce them.

Here was no Wine to be had; but as I carried with me a few Lemons in a Net, I drank some small Punch for Refreshment. When my Servant was preparing the Liquor,

my Landlord came to me, and asked me
seriously if those were Apples he was squeez-
ing.   And indeed there are as many Lemon-
Trees as Apple-Trees in that Country, nor
have they any Kind of Fruit in their Glens
that I know of.

Their Huts are mostly built on some rising
rocky Spot at the Foot of a Hill, secure from
any Bourne or Springs that might descend
upon them from the Mountains; and, thus
situated, they are pretty safe from Inundations
from above or below, and other Ground they
cannot spare from their Corn.   And even
upon the Skirts of the Highlands, where the
Laird has indulged two or three Trees from
his House, I have heard the Tenant lament
the Damage done by the Droppings and
Shade of them, as well as the Space taken up
by the Trunks and Roots.

The only Fruit the Natives have, that I
have seen, is the Bilberry, which is mostly
found near Springs, in Hollows of the Heaths.
The Taste of them to me is not very agree-

able, but they are much esteemed by the Inhabitants, who eat them with their Milk : yet in the Mountain-Woods, which for the most Part, are distant and difficult of Access, there are Nuts, Raspberries, and Strawberries; the two last, though but small, are very grateful to the Taste; but those Woods are so rare (at least it has always appeared so to me) that few of the Highlanders are near enough to partake of the Benefit.

I now set out on my last Stage, of which I had gone about five Miles, in much the same Manner as before, when it began to rain below, but it was Snow above to a certain Depth from the Summits of the Mountains. In about half an Hour afterwards, at the End of near a Mile, there arose a most violent Tempest. This, in a little Time, began to scoop the snow from the Mountains, and made such a furious Drift, which did not melt as it drove, that I could hardly see my Horse's head.

The Horses were blown aside from Place to Place as often as the sudden Gusts came on, being unable to resist those violent Eddy-Winds; and, at the same Time, they were nearly blinded with the Snow.

Now I expected no less than to perish, was hardly able to keep my Saddle, and, for Increase of Misery, my Guide led me out of the Way, having entirely lost his Landmarks.

When he perceived his Error he fell down on his Knees, by my Horse's Side, and in a beseeching Posture, with his Arms extended and in a howling Tone, seemed to ask Forgiveness.

I imagined what the Matter was (for I could but just see him, and that too by Fits), and spoke to him with a soft Voice, to signify I was not in Anger; and it appeared afterwards that he expected to be shot, as they have a dreadful Notion of the English.

Thus finding himself in no Danger of my Resentment, he addressed himself to the searching about for the Way from which he had deviated, and in some little Time I heard a

Cry of Joy, and he came and took my Horse by the Bridle, and never afterwards quitted it till we came to my new Lodging, which was about a Mile, for it was almost as dark as Night. In the mean Time I had given Directions to my Man for keeping close to my Horse's Heels; and if any Thing should prevent it, to call to me immediately, that I might not lose him.

As good Luck would have it, there was but one small River in the Way, and the Ford, though deep and winding, had a smooth, sandy Bottom, which is very rare in the Highlands.

There was another Circumstance favourable to us (I shall not name a third as one, which is our being not far from the Village, for we might have perished with Cold in the Night as well near it as further off), there had not a very great Quantity of Snow fallen upon the Mountains, because the Air began a little to clear, though very little, within about a Quarter of a Mile of the Glen, otherwise we might have been buried in some Cavity hid from us by the Darkness and the Snow.

But if this Drift, which happened to us upon some one of the wild Moors, had continued, and we had had far to go, we might have perished, notwithstanding the Knowledge of any Guide whatever.

These Drifts are, above all other Dangers, dreaded by the Highlanders; for my own Part, I could not but think of Mr. Addison's short Description of a Whirlwind in the wild, sandy Deserts of Numidia.

LETTER XVIII.

EVERY high Wind, in many Places of the Highlands, is a Whirlwind. The agitated Air, pouring into the narrow and high Spaces between the Mountains, being confined in its Course, and, if I may use the Expression, pushed on by a crowding Rear, till it comes to a bounded Hollow, or Kind of Amphitheatre; —I say, the Air, in that violent Motion, is there continually repelled by the opposite Hill, and rebounded from others, till it finds a Passage, insomuch that I have seen, in the Western Highlands, in such a Hollow, some scattering Oaks, with their Bark twisted almost as if it had been done with a Lever.

This, I suppose, was effected when they were young, and consequently the rest of their Growth was in that Figure : and I myself have met with such Rebuffs on every Side, from the Whirling of such Winds, as are not easy to be described.

When I came to my Inn, (you will think the Word a Burlesque), I found it a most wretched Hovel, with several pretty large Holes in the sides; and, as usual, exceedingly smoky.

My Apartment had a Partition about four Feet high, which separated it from the Lodging of the Family; And, being entered, I called for Straw or Heather to stop the Gaps. Some Straw was brought; but no sooner was it applied than it was pulled away on the outside.

This put me in a very ill Humour, thinking some malicious Highlander did it to plague or affront me; and, therefore, I sent my Man (who had just housed his Horses, and was helping me) to see who it could be; and immediately he returned laughing, and told me it was a poor hungry Cow, that was got to the Backside of the Hut for Shelter, and was pulling out the Straw for Provender.

The Smoke being something abated, and the Edifice repaired, I began to reflect on the miserable State I had lately been in; and esteemed that very Hut, which at another Time I should have greatly despised, to be to me as good as a Palace; and, like a keen Appetite with ordinary Fare, I enjoyed it accordingly, not envying even the Inhabitants of Buckingham-House.

Here I conclude my Journal, which I fear you will think as barren and tedious as the Ground I went over; but I must ask your Patience a little while longer concerning it, as no great reason yet appears to you why I should come to this wretched Place, and go no further.

By a Change of the Wind, there happened to fall a good deal of Rain in the Night; and I was told by my Landlord the Hills presaged more of it, that a wide River before me was become impassable, and if I remained longer in the Hills at that Season of the Year, I might be shut in for most Part of the

Winter ; for if fresh Snow should fall, and lie lower down on the Mountains than it did the Day before, I could not repass the Precipice, and must wait till the Lake was frozen so hard as to bear my Horses : and even then it was dangerous in those Places where the Springs bubble up from the Bottom, and render the Ice thin and incapable to bear any great Weight: —but that, indeed, those weak Spots might be avoided by Means of a skilful Guide.

As to the narrow Path, he said, he was certain that any Snow which might have lodged on it from the Drift was melted by the Rain which had then ceased. To all this he added a Piece of News (not very prudently, as I thought), which was, that some time before I passed the Precipice, a poor Highlander leading over it his Horse laden with *Creels*, or small Panniers, one of them struck against the upper Part of the Hill, as he supposed ; and whether the Man was endeavouring to save his Horse, or how it was, he could not tell, but that they both fell and were dashed to Pieces among the Rocks.

This to me was very affecting, especially as I was to pass the same Way in my Return.

Thus I was prevented from meeting a Number of Gentlemen of a Clan, who were to have assembled in a Place assigned for our Interview, about a Day and a half's Journey further in the Hills; and on the other side of the River were Numbers of Highlanders waiting to conduct me to them. But I was told, before I entered upon this Peregrination, that no Highlander would venture upon it at that Time of the Year; yet I piqued myself upon following the unreasonable Directions of such as knew nothing of the Matter.

Now I returned with as hasty Steps as the Way you have seen would permit, having met with no more Snow or Rain till I got into the lower Country; and then there fell a very great *Storm*, as they call it—for by the word *Storm*, they only mean Snow. And you may believe I then hugged myself, as being got clear of the Mountains.

But before I proceed to give you some Account of the Natives, I shall in Justice, say something relating to Part of the Country of Athole, which, though Highlands, claims an Exception from the preceding general and gloomy Descriptions; as may likewise some other Places, not far distant from the Borders of the Lowlands, which I have not seen.

This Country is said to be a Part of the ancient Caledonia. The Part I am speaking of is a Tract of Land, or *Strath*, which lies along the Sides of the Tay, a capital River of the Highlands.

The Mountains, though very high, have an easy Slope a good Way up, and are cultivated in many Places, and inhabited by Tenants who, like those below, have a different Air from other Highlanders in the Goodness of their Dress and Cheerfulness of their Countenances.

The Strath, or Vale, is wide and beautifully adorned with Plantations of various Sorts of Trees: the Ways are smooth, and in one Part, you ride in pleasant Glades, in another you have an agreeable Vista. Here you pass through Corn-Fields, there you ascend a small Height, from whence you have a pleasing Variety of that wild and spacious River, Woods, Fields, and neighbouring Mountains, which altogether give a greater Pleasure than the most Romantic Descriptions in Words, heightened by a lively Imagination, can possibly do; but the Satisfaction seemed beyond Expression, by comparing it in our Minds with the rugged Ways and horrid Prospects of the more northern Mountains, when we passed southward from them, through this Vale to the Low-Country ; but with respect to Athole in general, I must own that some Parts of it are very rugged and dangerous.

I shall not pretend to give you, as a People, the Original of the Highlanders, having no certain Materials for that Purpose; and, indeed, that Branch of History, with Respect even to Commonwealths and Kingdoms, is generally either obscured by Time, falsified by Tradition, or rendered fabulous by Invention ; nor do I think it would be of any great Importance, could I trace them up to their Source with Certainty; but I am persuaded they came from Ireland, in regard their Language is a Corruption of the Irish Tongue.

Spenser, in his "View of the State of Ireland," written in the Reign of Queen Elizabeth, sets forth the Dress and Customs of the Irish; and, if I remember right, they were, at that Time, very near what the People are now in the Highlands. But this is by the bye, as having little Relation to Antiquity; for Dress is variable, and Customs may be abolished by Authority; but Language will baffle the Efforts even of a Tyrant.

The Highlanders are exceedingly proud to be thought an unmixed People, and are apt to upbraid the English with being a Composition of all Nations; but, for my own Part, I think a little Mixture in that Sense would do themselves no Manner of Harm.

The Stature of the better Sort, so far as I can make the Comparison, is much the same with the English, or Low-Country Scots, but the common People are generally small; nor is it likely that, by being half-starved in the Womb, and never afterwards well fed, they should by that Means be rendered larger than other People.

How often have I heard them described in London as almost Giants in Size! and certainly there are a great many tall Men of them in and about that City; but the Truth is, when a young Fellow of any Spirit happens (as Kite says) to be born to be a *great Man*, he leaves the Country, to put himself into some foreign Service (chiefly in the Army), but the short ones are not commonly seen in other Countries than their own. I have seen a Hundred of them together come down to the Lowlands for Harvest-Work, as the Welsh come to England for the same Purpose, and but few sizeable Men among them; their Women are generally very small.

It has been said, likewise, that none of them are deformed by Crookedness: it is true, I have not seen many; for, as I observed of the People bordering upon the Highlands, none are spoiled by over Care of their Shapes. But is it to be supposed that Children who are left to themselves, when hardly able to go alone, in such a rugged Country, are free from all Accidents? Assertions so general are Ridiculous. They are also said to be very healthy and free from Distempers, notwithstanding the great Hardships they endure. Surely an Account of that Country from a Native is not unlike a Gascon's Account of himself. I own they are not very subject to Maladies occasioned by Luxury, but very liable to Fluxes, Fevers, Agues, Coughs, Rheumatisms, and other Distempers, incident to their Way of living; especially upon the Approach of Winter, of which I am a Witness.

By the Way, the poorer Sort are persuaded that Wine, or strong Malt Drink, is a very good Remedy in a Fever; and though I never prescribed either of them, I have administered both with as good Success as any Medicines prescribed by Doctor Radcliffe.

Æsculapius, even as a God, could hardly have had a more solemn Act of Adoration paid him than I had lately from a Highlander, at whose hut I lay in one of my Journeys. His Wife was then desperately ill of a Fever, and I left a Bottle of *Château Margoút* behind me to comfort her, if she should recover; for I had then several Horses laden with Wine and Provisions, and a great Retinue of Highlanders with me.

The poor Man fell down on his Knees in this dirty Street, and eagerly kissed my Hand; telling me, in Irish, I had cured his Wife with my good Stuff. This caused several Jokes from my Countrymen who were present, upon the poor Fellow's Value for his Wife; and the Doctor himself did not escape their Mirth upon that Occasion.

Having, Yesterday, proceeded thus far in my Letter, in order to have the less Writing this Evening, I had a Retrospection in the Morning to my Journal; and could not but be of Opinion that some few Additions were necessary to give you a clearer Notion of the inner Part of the Country, in regard to the incidents, in that Account, being confined to one short Progress, which could not include all that is wanting to be known for the Purpose intended.

There are few Days pass without some Rain or Snow in the Hills, and it seems necessary it should be so (if we may suppose Nature ever intended the worst Parts as Habitations for human Creatures), for the soil is so shallow and stony, and in Summer the Reflection of the Sun's Heat from the Sides of the Rocks is so strong, by Reason of the Narrowness of the Vales—to which may be added the Violent Winds—that otherwise the little Corn they have would be entirely dried and burnt up for want of proper Moisture.

The Clouds in their Passage often sweep along beneath the Tops of the high Mountains, and, when they happen to be above them, are drawn, as they pass, by Attraction, to the Summits, in plain and visible Streams and

Streaks, where they are broke, and fall in vast Quantities of Water. Nay, it is pretty common in the high Country for the Clouds, or some very dense Exhalation, to drive along the Part which is there called the Foot of the Hills, though very high above the Level of the Sea ; and I have seen, more than once, a very fair Rainbow described, at not above thirty or forty Yards' Distance from me, and seeming of much the same Diameter, having each Foot of the Semicircle upon the Ground.

An English Gentleman, one Day, as we stopped to consider this Phenomenon, proposed to ride into the Rainbow ; and though I told him the fruitless Consequence, since it was only a Vision made by his Eye, being at that Distance ; having the Sun directly behind, and before him the thick Vapour that was passing along at the Foot of the Hill ; yet (the Place being smooth) he set up a Gallop, and found his Mistake, to my great Diversion with him afterwards, upon his Confession that he had soon entirely lost it.

I have often heard it told by Travellers, as a Proof of the Height of Teneriffe, that the Clouds sometimes hide Part of that Mountain, and at the same Time the Top of it is seen above them : nothing is more ordinary than this in the Highlands. But I would not, therefore, be thought to insinuate, that these are as high as that ; but they may, you see, be brought under the same Description.

Thus you find the immediate Source of the Rivers and Lakes in the Mountains is the Clouds, and not as our Rivers, which have their Original from subterraneous Aqueducts, that rise in Springs below : but, among the Hills, the Waters fall in great Cascades and vast Cataracts, and pass with prodigious Rapidity through large rocky Channels, with such a Noise as almost deafens the Traveller whose Way lies along by their Sides. And when these Torrents rush through Glens or wider Straths, they often plough up, and sweep away with them, large Spots of the Soil, leaving nothing behind but Rock or

Gravel, so that the Land is never to be recovered. And for this a proportionable Abatement is made in the Tenant's Rent.

˙ The Lakes are very differently situated, with Respect to high and low. There are those which are vast Cavities filled up with Water, whereof the Surface is but little higher than the Level of the Sea; but of a surprising Depth. As Lake Ness, for the purpose, which has been ignorantly held to be without a Bottom; but was sounded by an experienced Seaman, when I was present, and appeared to be one hundred and thirty Fathoms or two hundred and sixty Yards deep.

It seems to be supplied by two small Rivers at its Head; but the great Increase of Water is from the Rivers, Bourns, and Cascades from the high Mountains at which it is bounded at the Water's Edge. And it has no other visible Issue but by the River Ness, which is not large; nor has the Lake any perceptible Current, being so spacious, as

more than a Mile in Breadth and twenty-one
in Length. At a Place called Foyers, there
is a steep Hill close to it, of about a quarter
of a Mile to the Top, from whence a River
pours into the Lake, by three successive wild
Cataracts, over romantic Rocks ; whereon, at
each Fall, it dashes with such Violence, that
in windy Weather the Side of the Hill is hid
from Sight for a good Way together by the
Spray, which looks like a thick Body of Smoke.
This Fall of Water has been compared with
the Cataracts of the Tiber, by those who have
seen them both.

There are other Lakes in large Hollows,
on the Tops of exceedingly high Hills ;—I
mean, they seem to any one below, who has
only heard of them, to be on the utmost
Height. But this is a Deception ; for there
are other Hills behind unseen, from whence
they are supplied with the great Quantity of
Water they contain. And it is impossible
that the Rain which Falls within the Compass
of one of those Cavities should not only be the

Cause of such a profound Depth of Water, but also supply the Drainings that descend from it, and issue out in Springs from the Sides of the Hills.

There are smaller Lakes, which are also seated high above the Plain, and are stored with Trout; though it seems impossible, by the vast Steepness of the Bourns on every visible Side, that those Fish should have got up thither from Rivers or Lakes below. This has often moved the Question,—" How came they there?" But they may have ascended by small Waters, in long Windings out of sight behind, and none steep enough to cause a Wonder; for I never found there was any Notion of their being brought thither for Breed. But I had like to have forgot that some will have them to have sprung from the Fry carried from other Waters, and dropped in those small Lakes by Water-Fowl.

In a Part of the Highlands called Strath-glass, there is a Lake too high by its Situation to be much affected by the Reflection of

Warmth from the Plain, and too low between
the Mountains, which almost join together, to
admit the Rays of the Sun ; for the only opening to it is on the North Side.   Here the Ice
continues all the Year round ; and though it
yields a little on the Surface to the Warmth
of the Circumambient Air by Day, in Summer-
Time, yet at the Return of Night it begins to
freeze as hard as ever.   This I have been
assured of, not only by the Proprietor himself,
but by several others in and near that Part of
the Country.

I have seen, in a rainy Day, from a Conflux
of Waters above, on a distant high Hill, the
Side of it covered over with Water by an
overflowing, for a very great Space, as you
may have seen the Water pour over the Brim
of a Cistern, or rather like its being covered
over with a Sheet ; and upon the peeping out
of the Sun the reflected Rays have dazzled my
Eyes to such a Degree, as if they were directed
to them by the Focus of a burning-Glass.

So much for the Lakes.

In one Expedition, where 1 was well attended, as I have said before, there was a River in my Way so dangerous that I was set upon the Shoulders of four Highlanders, my Horse not being to be trusted to in such Roughness, Depth, and Rapidity; and I really thought sometimes we should all have gone together. In the same Journey the Shoulders of some of them were employed to ease the Horses down from Rock to Rock; and all that long Day I could make out but nine Miles. This also was called a Road.

Toward the End of another Progress, in my Return to this Town, after several Hazards from increasing Waters, I was at Length stopped by a small River that was become impassable. There happened, luckily for me, to be a public Hut in this Place, for there was no going back again; but there was nothing to drink except the Water of the River. This I regretted the more, as I had refused, at one of the Barracks, to accept of a Bottle of Old Hock, on Account of the Carriage, and be-

II.   G

lieving I should reach hither before Night. In about three Hours after my Arrival at this Hut, there appeared, on the other Side of the Water, a Parcel of Merchants with little Horses loaded with Roundlets of Usky.

Within Sight of the Ford was a Bridge, as they called it, made for the Convenience of this Place; it was composed of two small Fir-Trees, not squared at all, laid, one beside the other, across a narrow Part of the River, from Rock to Rock: there were Gaps and Intervals between those Trees, and, beneath, a most tumultuous Fall of Water. Some of my Merchants, bestriding the Bridge, edged forwards, and moved the Usky Vessels before them; but the others, afterwards, to my Surprise, walked over this dangerous Passage, and dragged their *Garrons* through the Torrent, while the poor little Horses were almost drowned with the Surge.

I happened to have a few Lemons left, and with them I so far qualified the ill-Taste of the Spirit as to make it tolerable; but Eatables there were none, except Eggs and poor starved Fowls, as usual.

The Usky Men were my Companions, whom it was expected I should treat according to Custom, there being no Partition to separate them from me; and thus I passed a Part of the Day and great Part of the Night in the Smoke, and dreading the Bed: but my personal Hazards, Wants, and Inconveniences, among the Hills, have been so many, that I shall trouble you with no more of them, or very sparingly, if I do at all.

Some of the Bogs are of large Extent, and many People have been lost in them, especially after much rain in Time of Snow, as well as in the lesser *Mosses*, as they call them, where, in digging of Peat, there have been found Fir-Trees of a good magnitude, buried deep, and almost as hard as Ebony. This, like the Situation of the Mountains, is attributed to Noah's Flood, for they conclude the Trees have lain there ever since that Time, though it may be easily otherwise accounted for.   But what seems extraordinary to Strangers is, that there are often deep Bogs on the Declivities of Hills, and the higher you go the more you are bogged.

In a Part called Glengary, in my Return hither from the west Highlands, I found a Bog, or a Part of one, had been washed down by some violent Torrent from the Top of a Hill into the Plain, and the steep Slope was almost covered over with the muddy Substance that had rested there in its Passage downwards. This made a pretty deep Bog below, as a Gentleman who was with me found from his Curiosity to try it, being deceived by the Surface, which was dried by the Sun and Wind, for he forced his Horse into it, and sank, which surprised my Companion, who I thought, should have known better, being of Ireland.

I have heretofore hinted the Danger of being shut in by Waters, and thereby debarred from all Necessaries of Life, but have not yet mentioned the Extent of the Hills that intervene

between one Place of Shelter and another;
and indeed it is impossible to do so in general;
for they are sometimes nine or ten Scots
Miles over, and one of them in particular that
I have passed is Eighteen, wherein you frequently meet with Rivers, and deep, rugged
Channels in the Sides of the Mountains, which
you must pass, and these last are often the
most dangerous of the two; and both, if continued Rains should fall, become impassable
before you can attain the End, for which a
great deal of Time is required, by the Stoni-
ness and other Difficulties of the Way.
There is, indeed, one Alleviation; that as
these Rivers may, from being shallow, become
impracticable for the tallest Horse in two or
three Hours Time, yet will they again be passable, from their Velocity, almost as soon, if
the Rain entirely cease. When the Highlanders speak of these Spaces they call them
"Monts, without either House or Hall;" and
never attempt to pass them, if the Tops of
the Mountains presage bad Weather; yet in

that they are sometimes deceived by a sudden Change of Wind.

All this Way you may go without seeing a Tree, or coming within two Miles of a Shrub; and when you come at last to a small Spot of arable Land, where the rocky Feet of the Hills serve for Enclosure, what Work do they make about the Beauties of the Place, as though one had never seen a Field of Oats before!

You know that a polite Behaviour is common to the Army; but as it is impossible it should be universal, considering the different Tempers and other Accidents that atten Mankind, so we have here a certain Captain, who is almost illiterate, perfectly rude, and thinks his Courage and Strength are sufficient Supports to his Incivilities.

This Officer finding a Laird at one of the public Huts in the Highlands, and both going the same Way, they agreed to bear one another Company the Rest of the Journey. After they had ridden about four Miles, the

Laird turned to him, and said, "Now all the Ground we have hitherto gone over is my own Property."—"By G—!" says the other, "I have an Apple-Tree in Herefordshire that I would not swop with you for it all."

But to give you a better Idea of the Distance between one inhabited Spot and another, in a vast Extent of Country (Main and Island), I shall acquaint you with what a Chief was saying of his *Quondam* Estate. He told me, that if he was reinstated, and disposed to sell it, I should have it for the Purchase-Money of Three-pence an Acre.

I did not then take much Notice of what he said, it being at a Tavern in Edinburgh, and pretty late at Night, but, upon this Occasion of writing to you, I have made some Calculation of it, and find I should have been in Danger to have had a very bad Bargain. It is said to have been reduced by a Survey to a rectangle Parallelogram, or oblong Square, of sixty Miles by forty, which is 2,400 square Miles and 1,951,867 square Acres. It is called 1,500*l.* a-Year rent, but the Collector said he never received 900*l.*

Now the aforesaid Number of Acres, at 3*d.* per Acre, amounts to 24,398*l.* 6*s.* 9d.— and 900*l. per Annum*, at twenty-five Years' Purchase, is but 22,500*l.* ; the Difference is 1,896*l.* 6*s.* 9*d.*

There are other Observations that might not be improper, but I shall now defer them, and continue my Account of the People, which has likewise been deferred in this Letter.

LETTER XIX.

THE Highlanders are divided into Tribes, or Clans, under Chiefs, or Chieftains, as they are called in the Laws of Scotland; and each Clan again divided into Branches from the main Stock, who have Chieftains over them. These are subdivided into smaller Branches of fifty or sixty Men, who deduce their Original from their particular Chieftains, and rely upon them as their more immediate Protectors and Defenders. But for better Distinction I shall use the Word Chief for the Head of a whole Clan, and the Principal of a Tribe derived from him I shall call a Chieftain.

The ordinary Highlanders esteem it the most sublime Degree of Virtue to love their Chief, and pay him a blind Obedience, although it be in Opposition to the Government, the Laws of the Kingdom, or even to the Law of God. He is their Idol; and as they profess to know no King but him (I was going further), so will they say they ought to do whatever he commands without Inquiry.

Next to this Love of their Chief is that of the particular Branch from whence they sprang; and, in a third Degree, to those of the whole Clan or Name, whom they will assist, right or wrong, against those of any other Tribe with which they are at Variance, to whom their Enmity, like that of exasperated Brothers, is most outrageous.

They likewise owe good Will to such Clans as they esteem to be their particular Well-wishers; and lastly, they have an Adherence one to another as Highlanders, in Opposition to the People of the Low-Country, whom they despise as inferior to them in Courage, and believe they have a Right to plunder them whenever it is in their Power. This last arises from a Tradition, that the Lowlands, in old Times were the Possession of their Ancestors.

If the Truth of this Opinion of theirs stood in Need of any Evidence, it might, in good Measure, be confirmed by what I had from a Highland Gentleman of my Acquaintance. He told me that a certain Chief of a considerable Clan, in rummaging lately an old Charter-Chest, found a Letter directed by another Chief to his Grandfather, who is therein assured of the immediate Restitution of his *Lifted*,—that is, stolen, Cows ; for that he (the Writer of the Letter) had thought they belonged to the Lowland Lairds of Murray, whose Goods and Effects ought to be a Prey to them all.

When I mentioned this Tradition, I had only in View the middling and ordinary High-landers, who are very tenacious of old Customs and Opinions ; and, by the Example I have given of a Fact that happened almost a Century ago, I would be understood that it is very pro-bable such a Notion was formerly entertained by some, at least, among those of the highest Rank.

The Chief exercises an arbitrary Authority

over his Vassals, determines all Differences and
Disputes that happen among them, and levies
Taxes upon extraordinary Occasions, such as
the Marriage of a Daughter, building a House,
or some Pretence for his Support and the
Honour of the Name.   And if any one should
refuse to contribute to the best of his Ability
he is sure of severe Treatment, and if he per-
sisted in his Obstinacy he would be cast out
of his Tribe by general Consent : but Instances
of this Kind have very rarely happened.

This Power of the Chiefs is not supported
by Interest, as they are Landlords, but as
lineally descended from the old Patriarchs, or
Fathers of the Families ; for they hold the same
Authority when they have lost their Estates,
as may appear from several, and particularly
one who commands in his Clan, though, at the
same Time, they maintain him, having nothing
left of his own.

On the other Hand, the Chief, even against
the Laws, is to protect his Followers, as they
are sometimes called, be they never so criminal.

He is their Leader in Clan Quarrels, must free the Necessitous from their Arrears of Rent, and maintain such who, by Accidents, are fallen to total Decay.

If, by Increase of the Tribe, any small Farms are wanting for the Support of such Addition, he splits others into lesser Portions, because all must be somehow provided for ; and as the meanest among them pretend to be his Relations by Consanguinity, they insist upon the Privilege of taking him by the Hand wherever they meet him.

Concerning this last, I once saw a Number of very discontented Countenances when a certain Lord, one of the Chiefs, endeavoured to evade this Ceremony. It was in Presence of an English Gentleman in high Station, from whom he would willingly have concealed the Knowledge of such seeming Familiarity with Slaves of so wretched Appearance, and thinking it, I suppose, as a Kind of Contradiction to what he had often boasted at other Times, viz. his despotic Power in his Clan.

The unlimited Love and Obedience of the Highlanders to their Chiefs are not confined to the lower Order of their Followers, but are the same with those who are near them in Rank. As for Instance :—As I was travelling in a very wild Part of the Country, and approaching the House of one of those Gentlemen, who had Notice of my coming, he met me at some Distance from his Dwelling, with his Arcadian Offering of Milk and Cream, as usual carried before him by his Servants. He afterwards invited me to his Hut, which was built like the others, only very long, but without any Partition, where the Family was at one End, and some Cattle at the other. By the Way (although the Weather was not warm), he was without Shoes, Stockings, or Breeches, in a short Coat, with a Shirt not much longer, which hung between his Thighs, and just hid his Nakedness from two Daughters, about seventeen or eighteen Years old, who sat over against him. After some Compliments on either Side, and his wishing me *good Weather*, we entered into Conversation, in which he seemed to be a Man of as good Sense as he was well-proportioned. In speaking of the Country, he told me he knew I wondered how any Body would undergo the Inconveniences of a Highland Life.

You may be sure I was not wanting in an agreeable Contradiction, by saying I doubted not that they had their Satisfactions and Pleasures to countervail any Inconveniences they might sustain, though, perhaps, those Advantages could not be well known to such as are *en passant.* But he very modestly interrupted me as I was going on, and said he knew that what I said was the Effect of Complaisance, and could not be the real Sentiment of one who knew a good deal of the Country : " But," says he, " the Truth is, we are insensibly inured to it by Degrees; for, when very young, we know no better ; being grown up, we are inclined, or persuaded by our near Re- lations, to marry—thence come Children, and Fondness for them : but above all," says he, "is the *Love of our Chief*, so strongly is it inculcated to us in our Infancy; and, if it were not for that, I think the Highlands would be much thinner of People than they now are." By this, and many other Instances, I am fully persuaded, that the Highlanders are at least as fond of the Race of their Chiefs as a Frenchman is of the House of Bourbon

Several Reasons have just now offered themselves to me, in Persuasion to conceal one Circumstance of this Visit, but your Interest with me has prevailed against them all.

The two young Ladies, in my saluting them at parting, did me a Favour which with you would be thought the utmost Invitation; but it is purely innocent with them, and a Mark of the highest Esteem for their Guest. This was no great Surprise to me, having received the same Compliment several Times before in the Highlands, and even from married Women, who I may be sure had no further Design in it; and, like the two above-mentioned young Women, could never expect to see me again;

but I am not singular, for several Officers in the Army have told me they had received the same Courtesy from other Females in the Hills.

Some of the Chiefs have not only personal Dislikes and Enmity to each other, but there are also hereditary Feuds between Clan and Clan, which have been handed down from one Generation to another for several Ages.

These Quarrels descend to the meanest Vassal; and thus, sometimes, an innocent Person suffers for Crimes committed by his Tribe at a vast distance of Time before his Being began.

When a Quarrel begins in Words between two Highlanders of different Clans, it is esteemed the very Height of Malice and Rancour, and the greatest of all Provocations, to reproach one another with the Vices or personal Defects of their Chief, which, for the most Part, ends in Wounds or Death.

Often the Monuments of a Clan Battle, or some particular Murder, are the Incitements to great Mischiefs. The first-mentioned are small

II.   H

Heaps of Stones, thrown together on the Place where every particular Man fell in Battle; the other is from such a Heap first cast upon the Spot where the Fact was committed, and afterwards by Degrees increased to a high Pyramid, by those of the Clan that was wronged, in still throwing more Stones upon it as they pass by. The former I have seen overgrown with Moss, upon wide Moors, which showed the Number of Men that were killed in the Action. And several of the latter I have observed in my Journeys, that could not be less than fourteen or fifteen Feet high, with a Base proportionable. Thus, if several Men of Clans at Variance, happen to meet in View of one of these Memorials, 'tis odds but one Party reproaches the other with all the aggravating Circumstances that Tradition (which is mostly a Liar, either in the whole or a Part) has added to the original Truth; and then some great Mischief ensues. But if a single Highlander of the Clan that offended, should be met by two or three more of the others, he is sure to

be insulted, and receive some cruel Treatment
from them.

Thus these Heaps of Stones, as I have
heard an old Highlander complain, continue
to occasion the Revival of Animosities that
had their beginning perhaps Hundreds of
Years before any of the Parties accused
were Born : and therefore I think they ought,
by Authority, to be scattered, and effectually
defaced. But some of these Monuments have
been raised in Memory of such as have lost
their Lives in a Journey, by Snow, Rivers, or
other Accidents ; as was the Practice of the
eastern Nations.

By an old Scotish Law, the Chief was made
accountable for any Depredations or other
Violences committed by his Clan upon the
Borders of the Lowlands ; and in extraordinary
Cases he was obliged to give up his Son, or
some other nearest Relation, as a Hostage, for
the peaceable Behaviour of his Followers in
that Respect.

By this Law (for I never saw the Act), he

must surely have had an entire Command over them, at least tacitly, or by Inference understood. For how unreasonable, not to say unjust, must such a Restriction have been to him, if by Sanction of the same Law he had not had a coercive and judicial Authority over those, in whose Choice and Power it always lay to bring Punishment upon him? And if he had such an absolute Command over them, was it not to make of every Chief a petty Prince in his own Territory, and his Followers a People distinct and separate from all others?

For atrocious Crimes,—such as Rebellion, Murder, Rapes, or opposing the Execution of the Laws, which is also called Rebellion, when, by Process, the Chief or Laird was condemned in Absence, and *intercommuned*, as they call it, or outlawed,—the Civil Power, by Law and Custom, gave Letters of *Fire and Sword* against him; and the Officer of Justice might call for military Force to assist in the Execution. But, it is certain, some few of the Chiefs in former Times, were, upon Occasions, too powerful to be brought to Account by the Government. I have heard many Instances of the Faithfulness of particular Highlanders to their Masters, but shall relate only one, which is to me very well known.

At the Battle of Glenshiels, in the Rebellion of the Year 1719, a Gentleman (George Munroe of Culcairne), for whom I have a great esteem, commanded a Company of Highlandmen, raised out of his Father's Clan, and entertained at his own Expence. There he was dangerously wounded in the Thigh, from a Party of the Rebel Highlanders posted upon the Declivity of a Mountain, who kept on firing at him after he was down, according to their Want of Discipline, in spending much Fire upon one single Officer, which, distributed among the Body, might thin the Ranks of their Enemy.

When, after he fell, and found by their Behaviour they were resolved to dispatch him outright, he bid his Servant, who was by, get out of the Danger, for he might lose his Life, but could be of no Manner of Succour or

Service to him; and only desired him, that when he returned Home, he would let his Father and his Family know that he had not misbehaved. Hereupon the Highlander burst out into Tears; and asking him how he thought he could leave him in that Condition, and what they would think of him at Home, set himself down on his Hands and Knees over his Master, and received several Wounds, to shield him from further Hurt; till one of the Clan, who acted as a Serjeant, with a small Party, dislodged the Enemy, after having taken an Oath upon his Dirk that he would do it. For my own Part, I do not see how this Act of Fidelity is in any Way inferior to the so-celebrated one of Philocratus, Slave to Caius Gracchus, who likewise covered his Master with his Body, when he was found by his Enemies in a Wood, in such Manner that Caius could not be killed by them, till they had first dispatched his Domestic.

This Man had often waited at Table when his Master and I dined together, but otherwise is treated more like a Friend than a Servant.

The Highlanders, in order to persuade a Belief of their Hardiness, have several Rhodo-montades on that Head; for as the French Proverb says, *Tous les Gascons ne sont pas en France*—" There are vain Boasters in other Countries besides Gascony." It is true, they are liable to great Hardships, and they often suffer by them in their Health and Limbs, as I have often observed in a former Letter.

One of these Gasconades is, that the Laird of Keppoch, Chieftain of a branch of the M'Donalds, in a Winter Campaign against a neighbouring Laird, with whom he was at War about a Possession, gave Orders for rolling a Snow-Ball to lay under his Head in the Night; whereupon his Followers murmured, saying, " Now we despair of Victory, since our leader is become so effemi-nate he can't sleep without a Pillow." This and many other like Stories are romantic; but there is one Thing that at first Thought might seem very extraordinary, of which I have been credibly assured, that when the Highlanders are constrained to lie among the Hills in cold, dry, windy Weather, they sometimes soak the Plaid in some River or Bourn; and then holding up a Corner of it a little above their Heads, they turn themselves round and round, till they are enveloped by the whole Mantle. Then they lay themselves down on the Heath, upon the Leeward Side of some Hill, where the wet and the warmth of their Bodies make a Steam like that of a boiling Kettle. The wet they say keeps them warm by thickening the Stuff, and keeping the Wind from penetrating. I must confess I should myself have been apt to question this Fact, had I not frequently seen them wet from Morning to Night; and even at the Beginning of the Rain, not so much as stir a few Yards to shelter, but continue in it, without Necessity, till they were, as we say, wet through and through. And that is soon effected by the Looseness and Sponginess of the Plaiding;

but the Bonnet is frequently taken off, and wrung like a Dish-Clout, and then put on again. They have been accustomed from their Infancy to be often wet, and to take the Water like Spaniels; and this is become a second Nature, and can scarcely be called a Hardship to them, insomuch that I used to say, they seemed to be of the Duck Kind, and to love the Water as well. Though I never saw this Preparation for Sleep in windy Weather, yet, setting out early in a Morning from one of the Huts, I have seen the Marks of their Lodging, where the ground has been free from Rime or Snow, which remained all round the Spots where they had lain.

The different Surnames of the Highlanders in general are but few, in regard they are divided into large Families, and hardly any Male Strangers have intermarried with or settled among them; and with respect to particular Tribes, they commonly make that Alliance among themselves, who are all of one Name, except some few, may have affected to

annex themselves to the Clan, and those, for
the most Part, assume the Name [*without giving up their own.*]

Thus the Surnames, being useless for Distinction of Persons, are suppressed, and there
remain only the Christian Names; of which
there are everywhere a great Number of
Duncans, Donalds, Alexanders, Patricks, &c.,
who, therefore, must be some other Way
distinguished one from another. This is done
by some additional Names and Descriptions
taken from their Forefathers; for when their
own Christian Name, with their father's Name
and Description (which is for the most Part
the Colour of the Hair), is not sufficient, they
add the Grandfather's, and so upwards, till they
are perfectly distinguished from all others of
the same Clan-Name. As for Example, a Man
whose Name is *Donald Grant*, has for Patron-
ymic (as they call it) the Name following, viz.,

Donald Bane, *i.e.*	White-haired *Donald.*
Mac oil Vane,	Son of Grey-haird *Donald.*
Vic oil roi,	Grandson of red-haird *Donald.*
Vic ean,	Great-grandson to *John.*

Thus you see the Name of *Grant* is not used because of all that Clan are either so called, or assume that Name.

Another Thing is, that if this Man had descended in a direct Line, as eldest, from *John*, the remotest Ancestor, and *John* had been a Chief, he would only be called *Mac Ean*, leaving out all the intermediate Successions by Way of Eminence.

These patronymical Names, at length, are made use of Chiefly in Writings, Receipts, Rentals, &c. and, in ordinary Matters, the Highlanders have sometimes other Distinctions, which also to some are pretty long.

When Numbers of them, composed from different Tribes, have been jointly employed in a Work, they have had arbitrary and temporary Denominations added to their Christian Names by their Overseers, for the more ready Distinction; such as the Place they came from, the Person who recommended them, some particular Vice, or from something remarkable in their Persons, &c. by which

fictitious Names they have also been set down
in the Books of their Employers.

It is a received Notion (but nothing can be
more unjust) that the ordinary Highlanders
are an indolent, lazy People: I know the
Contrary by troublesome Experience;—I say
troublesome, because in a certain Affair wherein I had Occasion to employ great Numbers
of them, and gave them good Wages, the
Solicitations of others for Employment were
very earnest, and would hardly admit of a
Denial: they are as willing as other People
to mend their Way of Living; and, when
they have gained Strength from substantial
Food, they work as well as others; but why
should a People be branded with the Name
of Idlers, in a Country where there is generally no profitable Business for them to do?

Hence I have concluded, that if any
Expedient could be found for their Employment, to their reasonable Advantage, there
would be little else wanting to reform the
Minds of the most savage amongst them.

For my own Part, I do assure you, that I never had the least Reason to complain of the Behaviour towards me of any of the ordinary Highlanders, or the Irish; but it wants a great deal that I could truly say as much of the Englishmen and Lowland Scots that were employed in the same Business.

One of the Chiefs, at his own House, complained to me, but in a friendly Manner, as though I had seduced some of his Subjects from their Allegiance: he had Occasion for three or four of those of his Clan, whom I employed about a Piece of Work at Home, which they only could do; and, when he was about to pay them for their Labour, he offered them Six-pence a-Day each (being great Wages, even if they had not been his vassals), in Consideration he had taken them from other Employment; upon which they remonstrated, and said he injured them, in calling them from Sixteen-pence a-Day to Six-pence; and I very well remember he then told me that if any of those People had formerly said as much to their Chief, they would have been carried to the next Rock and precipitated.

The Highlanders walk nimbly and upright, so that you will never see, among the meanest of them, in the most remote Parts, the clumsy, stooping Gait of the French *Paisans*, or our own Country-Fellows, but, on the contrary, a kind of Stateliness in the Midst of their Poverty; and this I think may be accounted for without much Difficulty.

They have a Pride in their Family, as almost every one is a Genealogist: they wear light Brogues, or Pumps, and are accustomed to skip over Rocks and Bogs: whereas our Country Labourers have no such Pride, wear heavy, clouted Shoes, and are continually dragging their Feet out of ploughed Land or Clays; but those very Men, in a short Time after they are enlisted into the Army, erect their Bodies, change their clownish Gait, and become smart Fellows; and, indeed, the Soldiers in general, after being a little accustomed to the Toils and Difficulties of the

Country, can, and do, to my Knowledge,
acquit themselves, in their Winter-Marches
and other Hardships, as well as the Highlanders. On the other hand, it is observed
that the private Men of the independent Highland Companies are become less hardy than
others, from their great pay (as it is to them),
the best Lodging the Country affords, and
warm Clothing.

I cannot forbear to tell you, before I conclude, that many of those *private Gentlemen*
have *Gillys*, or Servants to attend them in
Quarters, and upon a March to carry their
Provisions and Firelocks; but, as I have happened to touch upon those Companies, it may
not be amiss to go a little further, for I think
I have just room enough for it in this Sheet.

There are six of them, viz. three of one hundred Men, and three of sixty each, in all, four
hundred and eighty Men. These are chiefly
Tenants to the Captains; and one of the *Cen-
turions*, or Captains of a Hundred, is said to
strip his other Tenants of their best Plaids

wherewith to clothe his Soldiers against a Re-
view, and to commit many other Abuses of his
Trust. These Captains are all of them vying
with each other whose Company shall best
perform the manual Exercise ; so that four
hundred and eighty Men, besides the Changes
made among them, are sufficient to teach that
Part of the military Discipline throughout the
whole Highlands.

I am not a Prophet, nor the Son of a
Prophet, or even *second-sighted*, yet I foresee
that a Time may come when the Institution
of these Corps may be thought not to have
been the best of Policy. I am not unaware it
may be said, they are raised in order to
facilitate the *Disarming*, and they are useful
to prevent the Stealing of Cattle ; but both
those Reasons are not sufficient to alter my
Opinion of their Continuance.

LETTER XX.

THE Gentry may be said to be a handsome People, but the Commonalty much otherwise; one would hardly think, by their Faces, they were of the same Species, at least of the same Country, which plainly proceeds from their bad Food, Smoke at home, and Sun, Wind, and Rain abroad; because the young Children have as good Features as any I have seen in other Parts of the Island.

I have mentioned the Sun in this northern Climate as partly the Cause of their Disguise, for that, as I said before, in Summer, the Heat, by Reflection from the Rocks, is excessive; at the same Time, the Cold on the Tops of the Hills is so vast an Extreme as cannot be conceived by any but those who have felt the Difference, and know the Danger of so sudden a Transition from one to the other; and this likewise has its Effect upon them.

The ordinary Natives are, for the most Part, civil when they are kindly used, but most mischievous when much offended, and will hardly ever forgive a Provocation, but seek some open or secret Revenge, and, generally speaking, the latter of the two.

A Highland Town, as before mentioned, is composed of a few Huts for Dwellings, with Barns and Stables, and both the latter are of a more diminutive Size than the former, all irregularly placed, some one Way, some another, and, at any Distance, look like so many Heaps of Dirt; these are built in Glens and Straths, which are the Corn-Countries, near Rivers and Rivulets, and also on the sides of Lakes, where there is some arable Land for the Support of the Inhabitants: but I am now to speak of the Manner in which the lower Order of the Highlanders live, and shall begin with the Spring of the Year.

This is a bad Season with them, for then

T. Jefferys sculp

their Provision of Oatmeal begins to fail, and, for a Supply, they bleed their Cattle, and boil the Blood into Cakes, which, together with a little Milk and a short Allowance of Oatmeal, is their Food. It is true, there are small Trouts, or something like them, in some of the little Rivers, which continue in Holes among the Rocks, which are always full of Water, when the Stream has quite ceased for want of Rain; these might be a Help to them in this starving Season; but I have had so little Notion in all my Journeys that they made those Fish a Part of their Diet, that I never once thought of them as such till this Moment. It is likely they cannot catch them for want of proper Tackle, but I am sure they cannot be without them for want of Leisure. What may seem strange is, that they do not introduct Roots among them (as Potatoes for the Purpose); but the Land they occupy is so very little, they think they cannot spare any Part of it from their Corn, and the Landlord's Demand of Rent in Kind is another Objection.

You will perceive I am speaking only of the
poor People in the interior Parts of the Mountains; for near the Coast, all around them,
there are few confined to such diminutive
Farms, and the most necessitous of all may
share, upon Occasion, the Benefit of various
Kinds of Shell-fish, only for seeking and
fetching.

Their Cattle are much weakened by want
of sufficient Food in the preceding Winter, and
this immoderate Bleeding reduces them to so
low a Plight that in the Morning they cannot
rise from the Ground, and several of the Inhabitants join together to help up each other's
Cows, &c.

In Summer the People remove to the Hills,
and dwell in much worse Huts than those they
leave below; these are near the Spots of Grazing, and are called *Shealings*, scattered from
one another as Occasion requires. Every one
has his particular Space of Pasture, for which,
if it be not a Part of His Farm, he pays, as I
shall mention hereafter. Here they make their

Butter and Cheese. By the Way, I have seen some of the former with blueish Veins, made, as I thought, by the Mixture of Smoke, not much unlike to Castile Soap; but some have said it was a Mixture of Sheep's Milk which gave a Part of it that Tincture of Blue.

When the Grazing fails, the Highlanders return to their former Habitations, and the Cattle to pick up their Sustenance among the Heath, as before.

At other Times the Children share the Milk with the Calves, Lambs, and Kids; for they milk the Dams of them all, which keeps their young so lean that when sold in the Low-Country they are chiefly used, as they tell me, to make Soups withal; and when a Side of any one of these Kinds hangs up in our Market the least disagreeable Part of the Sight is the Transparency of the Ribs.

About the latter End of August, or the Beginning of September, the Cattle are brought into good Order by their Summer Feed, and the Beef is extremely swect and succulent, which, I suppose, is owing, in good Part, to their being reduced to such Poverty in the Spring, and made up again with new Flesh.

Now, the Drovers collect their Herds, and drive them to Fairs and Markets on the Borders of the Lowlands, and sometimes to the North of England; and in their Passage they pay a certain Tribute, proportionable to the Number of Cattle, to the Owner of the Territory they pass through, which is in lieu of all Reckonings for Grazing.

I have several times seen them driving great Numbers of Cattle along the Sides of the Mountains at a great Distance, but never, except once, was near them. This was in a Time of Rain, by a wide River, where there was a Boat to ferry over the Drovers. The Cows were about fifty in Number, and took the Water like Spaniels; and when they were in, their Drivers made a hideous Cry to urge them forwards: this, they told me, they did to keep the Foremost of them from turning about; for, in that Case, the rest would do the like, and then they would be in Danger, especially the weakest of them, to be driven away and drowned by the Torrent. I thought it a very odd Sight to see so many Noses and Eyes just above Water, and nothing of them more to be seen, for they had no Horns, and upon the Land they appeared in Size and Shape like so many large Lincolnshire Calves.

I shall speak of the Highland Harvest,— that is, the Autumn, when I come to the Article of their Husbandry. But nothing is more deplorable than the State of these People in Time of Winter. They are in that Season often confined to their Glens by swollen Rivers, Snow, or Ice in the Paths on the Sides of the Hills, which is accumulated by Drippings from the Springs above, and so, by little and little, formed into Knobs like a Stick of Sugar-candy, only the Parts are not angular like those, but so uneven and slippery no Foot can pass.

They have no Diversions to amuse them, but sit brooding in the Smoke over the Fire till their Legs and Thighs are scorched to an extraordinary Degree, and many have sore Eyes, and some are quite blind. This long Continuance in the Smoke makes them almost as black as Chimney-Sweepers; and when the Huts are not Water-tight, which is often the Case, the Rain that comes through the Roof and mixes with the Sootiness of the Inside, where all the Sticks look like Charcoal, falls in Drops like Ink. But in this Circumstance, the Highlanders are not very solicitous about their outward Appearance.

To supply the Want of Candles, when they have Occasion for more Light than is given by the Fire, they provide themselves with a Quantity of Sticks of Fir, the most resinous that can be procured: some of these are lighted and laid upon a Stone; and as the Light decays they revive it with fresh Fuel. But when they happen to be destitute of Fire, and none is to be got in the Neighbourhood, they produce it by rubbing Sticks together; but I do not recollect what Kind of Wood is fittest for that Purpose.

If a Drift of Snow, from the Mountains happens, and the same should be of any Continuance, they are thereby rendered completely Prisoners. In this Case, the Snow, being whirled from the Mountains and Hills, lodges in the Plains below, till sometimes it increases to a Height almost equal with the Tops of their Huts ; but then it is soon dissolved for a little Space round them, which is caused by the Warmth of the Fire, Smoke, Family, and Cattle within.

Thus are they confined to a very narrow Compass ; and, in the mean Time, if they have any out-lying Cattle in the Hills, they are leaving the Heights and returning Home : for by the same Means that the Snow is accumulated in the Glen, the Hills are cleared of the Incumbrance, but the Cattle are sometimes intercepted by the Depth of Snow in the Plain, or deep Hollows in their Way. In such Case, when the Wind's Drift begins to cease, from the Wind having a little spent its Fury, the People take the following Method to open a Communication :—if the Huts are at any Distance asunder, one of them begins at the Edge of the Snow next to his Dwelling, and, waving his Body from Side to Side, presses forward and squeezes it from him on either Hand; and if it be higher than his Head he breaks down that Part with his Hands. Thus he proceeds till he comes to another Hut, and when some of them are got together they go on in the same Manner to open a Way for the Cattle; and in thus doing they relieve one another, when too wet and weary to proceed further, till the whole is completed. Yet, notwithstanding all their Endeavours their Cattle are sometimes lost.

As this may seem to you a little too extra-ordinary, and you will believe I never saw it, I shall assure you I had it from a Gentleman, who, being nearly related to a Chief, has therefore a considerable Farm in the inner Highlands, and would not deceive me in a Fact that does not recommend his Country, of which he is as jealous as any one I have known on this Side the Tweed.

A Drift of Snow like that above described, was said to have been the Ruin of the Swedish Army, in the last Epedition of Charles XII.

Before I proceed to their Husbandry, I shall give you some Account of an Animal necessary to it ; that is, their Horses, or rather (as they are called) Garrons. These Horses in Miniature run wild among the Mountains ; some of them till they are eight or ten Years old, which renders them exceedingly restive and stubborn. There are various Ways of catching them, according to the Nature of the Spot of Country where they chiefly keep their Haunts. Sometimes they are hunted by Numbers of Highlandmen into a Bog ; in other Places they are driven up a steep Hill, where the nearest of the Pursuers endeavours to catch them by the hind-leg ; and I have been told, that sometimes both Horse and Man have come tumbling down together. In

another Place they have been hunted from
one to another, among the Heath and Rocks,
till they have laid themselves down through
Weariness and want of Breath.

They are so small that a middle-sized Man
must keep his Legs almost in Lines parallel to
their Sides when carried over the stony Ways;
and it is almost incredible to those who have
not seen it, how nimbly they skip with a heavy
Rider among the Rocks and large Moor-Stones,
turning Zig-Zag to such Places that are
passable.   I think verily they all follow one
another in the same irregular Steps, because
in those Ways there appears some little
Smoothness, worn by their naked Hoofs,
which is not anywhere else to be seen.   When
I have been riding or rather creeping along at
the Foot of a Mountain, I have discovered
them by their Colour, which is mostly white,
and, by their Motion, which readily catches
the Eye, when, at the same Time, they were
so high above me, they seemed to be no
bigger than a Lap-dog, and almost hanging

over my Head. But what has appeared to me very extraordinary is, what when at other Times, I have passed near to them, I have perceived them to be (like some of our common beggars in London) in ragged and tattered Coats, but full in flesh; and that, even toward the latter End of Winter, when I think they could have nothing to feed upon but Heath and rotten leaves of Trees if any of the latter were to be found. The Highlanders have a Tradition that they came originally from Spain, by Breeders left there by the Spaniards in former Times; and they say, they have been a great Number of Years dwindling to their present diminutive Size. I was one Day greatly diverted with the Method of taming these wild Hobbies.

In passing along a narrow Path, on the Side of a high Hill among the Mountains, at length it brought me to a Part looking down into a little Plain, there I was at once presented with the Scene of a Highlandman beating one of these Garrons, most unmercifully, with a great Stick; and, upon a stricter View,

I perceived the Man had tied a Rope, or something like it, about one of his hind-Legs, as you may have seen a single Hog driven in England ; and, indeed, in my Situation, he did not seem so big. At the same Time the Horse was kicking and violently struggling, and sometimes the Garron was down and sometimes the Highlander, and not seldom both of them together, but still the Man kept his Hold.

After waiting a considerable Time to see the Event, though not so well pleased with the Precipice I stood upon, I found the Garron gave it up ; and, being perfectly conquered for that Time, patiently suffered himself to be driven to a Hut not far from the field of Battle.

I was desirous to ask the Highlander a Question or two by the Help of my Guide, but there were no Means for me to get down but by falling ; and when I came to a Part of the Hill where I could descend to the Glen, I had but little Inclination to go back again, for

I never, by Choice, made one Retrograde Step when I was leaving the Mountains : but what is pretty strange, though very true (by what Charm I know not), I have been well enough pleased to see them again, at my first Entrance to them in my Returns from England ; and this has made my Wonder cease that a Native should be so fond of such a Country.

The Soil of the Corn-Lands is in some Places so shallow, with rocky Ground beneath it, that a Plough is of no Manner of Use. This they dig up with a wooden Spade ; for almost all their Implements of Husbandry, which in other Countries are made of Iron, or partly of that Metal, are, in some Parts of the Highlands, entirely made of Wood,—such as the Spade, Plough-share, Harrow, Harness, and Bolts ; and even Locks for Doors are made of Wood. By the Way, these Locks are contrived so artfully, by Notches made at unequal Distances within-side, that it is Impossible to open them with any Thing but the wooden Keys that belong to them. But there

would be no great Difficulty in opening the
Wall of the Hut, as the Highlander did by the
Portmanteau that he saw lying upon a Table,
and nobody near it but his Companion.
"Out!" says he; "what Fool was this that
put a Lock upon Leather?" and immediately
ripped it open with his Dirk.

Where the Soil is deeper they plough with
four of their Little Horses abreast. The Manner this:—Being thus ranked they are divided
by a small Space into Pairs, and the Driver,
or rather Leader, of the Plough, having placed
himself before them, holding the two inner-
most by their Heads to keep the Couples
asunder, he with his Face toward the Plough,
goes backward, observing, through the Space
between the Horses, the Way of the Plough-
share.

When I first saw this awkward Method
as I then thought it, I rode up to the
Person who guided the Machine, to ask him
some Questions concerning it: he spoke pretty
good English, which made me conclude he was

a Gentleman; and yet, in Quality of a Proprietor and Conductor, might, without Dishonour, employ himself in such a Work. My first Question was, whether that Method was common to the Highlands, or peculiar to that Part of the Country? and, by way of Answer, he asked me if they ploughed otherwise anywhere else. Upon my further Inquiry why the Man went Backwards? he stopped and very civilly informed me that there were several small Rocks, which I did not see, that had a little Part of them just peeping on the Surface, and therefore it was necessary his Servants should see and avoid them, by guiding the Horses accordingly, or otherwise his Plough might be spoiled by the Shock. The Answer was satisfactory and convincing, and I must here take Notice that many other of their Methods are too well suited to their own Circumstances, and those of the Country, to be easily amended by such as undertake to deride them.

In the Western Highlands they still retain that barbarous Custom (which I have not seen

II   K

anywhere else) of drawing the Harrow by the Horse's Dock, without any Manner of Harness whatever. And when the Tail becomes too short for the Purpose, they lengthen it out with twisted Sticks. This unnatural Practice was formerly forbidden in Ireland by Act of Parliament, as my Memory informs me, from Accounts I have formerly read of that Country for being almost without Books I can have little other Help wherefrom to make Quotations.

When a Burden is to be carried on Horseback they use two Baskets, called *Creels*, one on each Side of the Horse; and if the Load be such as cannot be divided, they put it into one of them, and counterbalance it with Stones in the other, so that one Half of the Horse's Burden is—I cannot say unnecessary, because I do not see how they could do otherwise in the Mountains.

Their Harvest is late in the Year, and therefore seldom got in dry, as the great Rains usually come on about the latter End of August: nor is the Corn well preserved after-

wards in those miserable Hovels they call
Barns, which are mostly not fit to keep out
the bad Weather from above; and were it not
for the high Winds that pass through the
Openings of the Sides in dry Weather, it
would of Necessity be quite spoiled. But as
it is, the Grain is often grown in the Sheaves,
as I observed in a former Letter.

To the Lightness of the Oats, one might
think they contributed themselves; for if there
be one Part of their Ground that produces
worse Grain than another, they reserve that, or
Part of it, for Seed, believing it will produce
again as well, in Quantity and Quality, as the
best; but, whether in this they are right or
wrong, I cannot determine.

Another Thing, besides the bad Weather,
that retards their Harvest, is, they make it
chiefly the Work of the Women of the Family.
Near the Lowlands I have known a Field of
Corn to employ a Woman and a Girl for a
Fortnight, which, with proper Help, might
have been done in two Days. And, although

the Owner might not well afford to employ
many Hands, yet his own Labour would have
prevented half the Risk of bad Weather at
that uncertain Season.

An English Lady, who found herself something decaying in her Health, and was advised
to go among the Hills, and drink Goat's Milk
or Whey, told me lately, that seeing a Highlander basking at the Foot of a Hill in his full
Dress, while his Wife and her Mother were
hard at work in reaping the Oats, she asked
the old Woman how she could be contented
to see her Daughter labour in that Manner
while her Husband was only an idle Spectator?
And to this the Woman answered, that her
Son-in-Law was a *Gentleman*, and it would be
a Disparagement to him to do any such Work;
and that both she and her Daughter too were
sufficiently honoured by the Alliance.

This Instance, I own, has something particular in it, as such; but the Thing is very
common, *à la Palatine,* among the middling
Sort of People.

Not long ago, a French Officer, who was coming hither the Hill Way, to raise some Recruits for the Dutch Service, met a Highlandman with a good Pair of Brogues on his Feet, and his Wife marching bare-foot after him. This Indignity to the Sex raised the Frenchman's Anger to such a Degree, that he leaped from his Horse, and obliged the Fellow to take off the Shoes, and the Woman to put them on.

By this last Instance (not to trouble you with others) you may see it is not in their Harvest-work alone they are something in the *Palatine* Way with Respect to their Women.

The Highlanders have a Notion that the Moon, in a clear Night, ripens their Corn much more than a Sun-shiny Day : for this they plead Experience ; yet they cannot say by what Rule they make the Comparison. But, by this Opinion of theirs, I think they have little Knowledge of the Nature of those two Planets.

In larger Farms, belonging to Gentlemen of the Clan, where there are any Number of Women employed in Harvest-Work, they all keep Time together, by several barbarous Tones of the Voice; and stoop and rise together as regularly as a Rank of Soldiers when they ground their Arms. Sometimes they are incited to their Work by the Sound of a Bagpipe; and by either of these they proceed with great Alacrity, it being disgraceful for any one to be out of Time with the Sickle. They use the same Tone, or a Piper, when they thicken the newly-woven Plaiding, instead of a Fulling-Mill.

This is done by six or eight Women sitting upon the Ground, near some River or Rivulet, in two opposite Ranks, with the wet Cloth between them; their Coats are tucked up, and with their naked Feet they strike one against another's, keeping exact Time as above-mentioned. And among Numbers of Men, employed in any Work that requires Strength and joint Labour (as the launching a large Boat, or the like), they must have the Piper to regulate their Time, as well as Usky to keep up their Spirits in the Performance; for Pay they often have little, or none at all.

Nothing is more common than to hear the Highlanders boast how much their Country might be improved, and that it would produce double what it does at present if better Husbandry were introduced among them. For my own Part, it was always the only Amusement I had in the Hills, to observe every minute Thing in my Way: and I do assure you, I do not remember to have seen the least Spot that would bear Corn uncultivated, not even upon the Sides of the Hills, where it could be no otherwise broke up than with a Spade. And as for Manure to supply the Salts and enrich the Ground, they have hardly any. In Summer their Cattle are dispersed about the *Sheelings*, and almost all the rest of the Year in other Parts of the Hills; and, therefore, all the Dung they can have must be from the trifling Quantity made by the Cattle while they are in the House. I never knew or heard of any Limestone, Chalk, or Marl, they have in the

Country; and, if some of their Rocks might
serve for Limestone, in that Case their Kilns,
Carriage, and Fuel would render it so expensive,
it would be the same Thing to them as if there
were none.   Their great Dependence is upon
the Nitre of the Snow; and they lament the
Disappointment if it does not fall early in the
Season.   Yet I have known, in some, a great
Inclination to Improvement; and shall only
instance a very small Matter, which, perhaps,
may be thought too inconsiderable to mention.

Not far from Fort William, I have seen
Women with a little Horse-Dung brought
upon their backs, in *Creels*, or Baskets, from
that Garrison; and, on their Knees, spreading
it with their Hands upon the Land, and even
breaking the Balls, that every Part of the little
Spot might have its due Proportion.

These Women have several Times brought
me Hay to the Fort, which was made from
Grass cut with a Knife by the Way-side; and
from one I have bought two or three Penny-

worth ; from another, the Purchase has been
a Groat ; but six-pennyworth was a most considerable Bargain.

At their Return from the Hay-Market, they
carried away the Dung of my Stable (which
was one End of a Dwelling-Hut) in the Manner
above-mentioned.

Speaking of Grass and Hay, it comes to my
Remembrance, that, in passing through a Space
between the Mountains, not far from Keppoch,
in Lochaber, I observed, in the Hollow, though
too narrow to admit much of the Sun, a greater
Quantity of Grass than I remembered to have
seen in any such Spot in the inner Parts of
the Highlands; it was in the Month of August,
when it was grown rank, and flagged pretty
much, and therefore I was induced to ask why
the Owner did not cut it. To this I was
answered, it never had been mowed, but was
left every Year as natural Hay for the Cattle
in Winter,—that is, to lie upon the ground
like Litter, and, according to their Description,
the Cows routed for it in the Snow, like Hogs

in a Dunghill.   But the People have no Barns
fit to contain a Quantity of Hay, and it would
be impossible to secure it in Mows from the
tempestuous eddy-Winds, which would soon
carry it over the Mountains : besides, it could
not well be made, by reason of Rains and want
of Sun, and therefore they think it best to
let it lie as it does, with the Roots in the
Ground.

The Advantage of Enclosures is a mighty
Topic with the Highlanders, though they cannot spare for Grass one Inch of Land that will
bear Corn ; if they could, it would be a much
more expensive Way of grazing their Cattle
than letting them run as they do in the Hills ;
but Enclosures, simply as such, do not better
the Soil, or, if they might be supposed to be
an Advantage to it, where is the Highland
Tenant that can lay out ten Shillings for that
Purpose ?   and what would he be the gainer
by it in the End, but to have his Rent raised,
or his Farm divided with some other ? or,
lastly, where are the Number of Highlanders

that would patiently suffer such an inconvenient Innovation? For my Part, I think Nature has sufficiently inclosed their Lands by the Feet of the surrounding Mountains. Now, after what has been said, where can this Improvement be? Yet, it seems, they had rather you should think them ignorant, lazy, or anything else, than entertain a bad Opinion of their Country. But I have dwelt too long upon this Head.

Their Rent is chiefly paid in Kind,—that is to say, great Part of it in several Species arising from the Product of the Farm; such as Barley, Oatmeal, and what they call *Customs*, as Sheep, Lambs, Poultry, Butter, &c., and the Remainder, if any, is paid in Money, or an Addition of some one of the before-mentioned Species, if Money be wanting.

The Gentlemen, who are near Relations of the Chief, hold pretty large Farms, if the Estate will allow it,—perhaps twenty or thirty Pounds a-Year, and they again, generally, parcel them out to under-Tenants in small Portions: hence it comes, that, by such a

Division of an old Farm (part of an upper-Tenant's Holding), suppose among eight Persons, each of them pays an eighth Part of every Thing, even to the Fraction of a Capon, which cannot in the Nature of it be paid in Kind, but the Value of it is cast in with the rest of the Rent, and, notwithstanding the above-mentioned Customs are placed in an upper-Tenant's Rental, yet they properly belong to the Chief, for the Maintenance of the Family in Provisions.

Every Year, after the Harvest, the Sheriff of the County, or his Deputy, together with a Jury of landed Men, set a Rate upon Corn-Provisions, and the Custom of the Country regulates the rest. The Sheriff's Regulation for the Year is called the *Feers-price*, and serves for a Standard whereby to determine everything relating to Rents and Bargains; so that if the Tenant is not provided with all the Species he is to pay, then that which is wanting may be converted into Money, or something else with Certainty.

Before I conclude this Letter, I shall take notice of one Thing, which, at first, I thought pretty extraordinary, and that is, if any land-d Man refuses, or fails to pay the King's Tax, then, by a Warrant from the Civil Magistrate, a proportionable Number of Soldiers are quartered upon him, with sometimes a Commissioned Officer to command them, all of whom he must maintain till the Cess is fully discharged. This is a Penalty for his Default, even though he had not the Means to raise Money in all that Time : and, let it be ever so long, the Tax in the End is still the same. You will not doubt that the Men, thus living upon free-Quarters, use the best Interests with their Officers to be sent on such Parties.

LETTER XXI.

YOU will, it is likely, think it strange that many of the Highland Tenants are to maintain a Family upon a Farm of twelve Merks Scots *per Annum*, which is thirteen Shillings and four-Pence sterling, with perhaps a Cow or two, or a very few Sheep or Goats; but often the Rent is less and the Cattle are wanting.

In some Rentals you may see seven or eight Columns of various Species of Rent, or more, viz. Money, Barley, Oatmeal, Sheep, Lambs, Butter, Cheese, Capons, &c.; but every Tenant does not pay all these Kinds, though many of them the greatest Part. What follows is a Specimen taken out of a Highland Rent-roll, and I do assure you it is genuine, and not the least by many :—

	Scots Money.			English.			Butter. Stones.	*lb.*	*oz.*	Oatmeal. *Bolls.*	*B.*	*P.*	*Lip.*	Muttons.
Donald mac Oil vic ille Challum,	£3	10	4	£0	5	10⅛	0	3	2	0	2	1	3	⅛ and $\frac{1}{16}$
Murdoch mac illi Christ, . .	5	17	6	0	9	9⅛	0	6	4	0	3	3	3	¼ and $\frac{1}{16}$
Duncan mac illi Phadrick, . .	7	0	6	0	12	3½	0	7	8	1	0	3	0½	¼ and ⅛

I shall here give you a Computation of the first Article, besides which there are seven more of the same Farm and Rent, as you may perceive by the Fraction of a Sheep in the last Column:—

The Money, ...	£0	5	10⅛ *Sterling.*
The Butter, three Pounds two Ounces, at 4d. per lb., .	0	1	1½
Oatmeal, 2 Bushels, 1 Peck, 3 Lippys and ¼, at 6d. per Peck,	0	4	9¼ and ½
Sheep, one-Eighth and one-Sixteenth, at 2s., . . .	0	0	4½
The yearly Rent of the Farm is . .	0	12	1½ and $\frac{1}{12}$

The Landlord has, by Law, an *Hypothic*, or right of Pledge, with respect to the Corn for so much as the current Year's Rent, and may, and often does, by himself or his Bailiff, see it reaped to his own Use ; or, if that is not done, he may seize it in the Market or anywhere else : but this last Privilege of the Landlord does not extend to the Crop or Rent of any former Year.

The Poverty of the Tenants has rendered it Customary for the Chief, or Laird, to free some of them, every Year, from all Arrears of Rent ; this is supposed, upon an Average to be about one Year in five of the whole Estate.

If the Tenant is to hire his Grazing in the Hills, he takes it by *Soumes ;*—a *Soume* is as much Grass as will maintain four Sheep; eight Sheep are equal to a Cow and a half, or forty Goats ; but I do not remember how much is paid for every *Soume*. The reason of this Disproportion between the Goats and Sheep is, that, after the Sheep have eaten the Pasture bare, the Herbs, as Thyme, &c. that are left behind, are of little or no Value, except for the Browsing of Goats.

The Laird's Income is computed by *Chalders* of Victuals, as they are called ;—a *Chalder* is sixteen Bolls of Corn, each Boll containing about six of our Bushels, and therefore, when any one speaks of the yearly Value of such a Laird's Estate, he tells you it is so many *Chalders ;* but the Measure varies something in different Parts of the Country.

When a Son is born to the Chief of a Family, there generally arises a Contention among the Vassals which of them shall have the fostering of the Child when it is taken from the Nurse ; and by this Means such Differences are sometimes fomented as are hardly ever after thoroughly reconciled. The happy Man who succeeds in his Suit is ever after called the Foster-Father, and his Children the Foster-brothers and Sisters, of the young Laird. This, they reckon, not only endears them to their Chief, and greatly strengthens their Interest with him, but gives them a great deal of

II.   L

Consideration among their Fellow-Vassals;
and the Foster-brother having the same Education as the young Chief, may, besides that,
in Time become his *Hanchman*, or perhaps be
promoted to that Office under the old Patriarch
himself, if a Vacancy should happen; or otherwise, by their Interest, obtain Orders and a
Benefice.   This Officer, is a Sort of Secretary,
and is to be ready, upon all Occasions, to venture his Life in Defence of his Master; and
at Drinking-bouts he stands behind his Seat, at
his Haunch, (from whence his Title is derived),
and watches the Conversation, to see if any
one offend his Patron.

An English Officer, being in Company with
a certain Chieftain and several other Highland
Gentlemen, near Killichumen, had an Argument with the *great Man;* and, both being
well warmed with Usky, at last the Dispute
grew very hot.   A Youth who was *Hanchman*, not understanding a Word of English,
imagined his Chief was insulted, and thereupon
drew his Pistol from his Side, and snapped it

at the Officer's Head ; but the Pistol missed
Fire, otherwise it is more than probable he
might have suffered Death from the Hand of
that little Vermin.   But it is very disagreeable
to an Englishman, over a Bottle with the
Highlanders, to see every one of them have
his *Gilly,*—that is, his Servant, standing behind him all the while, let what will be the
Subject of Conversation.

When a Chief goes a Journey in the Hills,
or makes a formal Visit to an Equal, he is said
to be attended by all, or most part of the
Officers following, viz.—

The Hanchman,	Before described.
Bard,	His Poet.
Bladier,	His Spokesman.
Gilli-more,	Carries his Broad-Sword.
Gilli-casflue,	Carries him when on Foot, over the Fords.
Gilly-constraine,	Leads his Horse in rough and dangerous Ways.
Gilly-trushanarnish,	The Baggage-Man.
The Piper,	Who, being a Gentleman, I should have named sooner.

And lastly,

The Piper's Gilly,	Who Carries the Bagpipe.

There are likewise some Gentlemen near of
Kin who bear him Company; and besides a
number of the common Sort, who have no particular Employment, but follow him only to
partake of the Cheer.

I must own that all these Attendants, and
the profound Respect they pay, must be
flattering enough, though the Equipage has
none of the best Appearance. But this *State*
may appear to soothe the Pride of the Chief
to a vast Degree, if the Declaration of one of
them was sincere, who, at Dinner, before a
good deal of Company, English as well as
Scots, myself being one of the Number,
affirmed that if his Estate was free from In-
cumbrances, and was none of his own, and he
was then put to choose between that and the
Estate of the Duke of Newcastle, supposing
it to be thirty thousand Pounds a-Year (as
somebody said it was), he would make Choice
of the former, with the *following* belonging to
it before the other without it. Now his
Estate might be about five hundred Pounds

a-Year. But this Pride is pretty costly; for as his Friend is to feed all these Attendants, so it comes to his own Turn to be at a like, or, perhaps, greater Expence when the Visit is repaid; for they are generally attended in Proportion to the Strength of the Clan; and by this Intercourse they very much hurt one another in their Circumstances.

By what has been said, you may know, in Part, how necessary the rent called *customs* is to the Family of a Highland Chief.

Here I must ask a Space for those two Sons of Apollo, the *Bard* and the *Piper*.

The *Bard* is skilled in the Genealogy of all the Highland Families; sometimes Preceptor to the young Laird; celebrates, in Irish Verse, the Original of the Tribe, the famous warlike Actions of the successive Heads, and sings his own Lyrics as an Opiate to the Chief when indisposed for Sleep;—but Poets are not equally esteemed and honoured in all Countries. I happened to be a Witness of the Dishonour done to the Muse at the House of one of the

Chiefs, where two of these Bards were set at
a good Distance, at the lower End of a long
Table, with a Parcel of Highlanders of no extraordinary Appearance, over a Cup of Ale.
Poor Inspiration! They were not asked to
drink a Glass of Wine at our Table, though
the whole Company at it consisted only of the
Great Man, one of his near Relations, and
myself.

After some little Time, the Chief ordered
one of them to sing me a Highland Song.
The Bard readily obeyed; and with a hoarse
Voice, and in a Tune of few various Notes,
began, as I was told, one of his own Lyrics;
and when he had proceeded to the fourth or
fifth Stanza, I perceived, by the Names of
several Persons, Glens, and Mountains, which
I had known or heard of before, that it was an
Account of some Clan Battle. But, in his
going on, the Chief (who piques himself upon
his School-Learning), at some particular Passage, bid him cease, and cried out to me—
"There's nothing like that in Virgil or Homer!"

I bowed, and told him I believed so. This, you may believe, was very edifying and delightful.

I have had Occasion before to say something of the *Piper*, but not as an Officer of the Household.

In a Morning, while the Chiet is dressing, he walks backward and forward, close under the Window, without Doors, playing on his Bagpipe, with a most upright Attitude and majestic Stride.

It is a Proverb in Scotland, viz. *The stately Step of a Piper.* When required, he plays at Meals, and in an Evening is to divert the Guests with his Music, when the Chief has Company with him : his Attendance in a Journey, or at a Visit I have mentioned before.

His *Gilly* holds the Pipe till he begins; and the Moment he has done with the Instrument, he disdainfully throws it down upon the Ground, as being only the passive Means of conveying his Skill to the Ear, and not a proper Weight for him to carry or bear at

other Times.   But, for a contrary Reason,
his Gilly snatches it up—which is, that the
Pipe may not suffer Indignity from its Neglect.

The Captain of one of the Highland Companies entertained me some Time ago at Stirling, with an Account of a Dispute that
happened in his *Corps* about Precedency.
This Officer, among the rest, had received
Orders to add a Drum to his Bagpipe, as a
more military Instrument; for the Pipe was to
be retained, because the Highlandmen could
hardly be brought to march without it.   Now,
the Contest between the Drummer and the
Piper arose about the Post of Honour, and at
length the Contention grew exceedingly hot,
which the Captain having Notice of, he called
them both before him, and, in the End, de-
cided the Matter in Favour of the Drum;
whereupon the Piper remonstrated very
warmly.   " Ads Wuds, sir," says he, "and
shall a little Rascal that beats upon a Sheep-
skin, tak the right Haund of me, that am a
Musician ?"

There are in the Mountains both red-Deer and Roes, but neither of them in very great Numbers, that ever I could find. The red-Deer are large, and keep their Haunts in the highest Mountains; but the Roe is less than our fallow-Deer, and partakes, in some Measure, of the Nature of the hare, having no Fat about the flesh, and hiding in the Clefts of Rocks, and other Hollows, from the Sight of Pursuers. These keep chiefly in the Woods.

A Pack of Hounds, like that of Actæon, in the same metaphorical Sense, would soon devour their Master. But, supposing they could easily be maintained, they would be of no Use, it being impossible for them to hunt over such Rocks and rugged steep Declivities; or if they could do this, their Cry in those open Hills would soon fright all the Deer out of that Part of the Country. This was the Effect of one single Hound, whose Voice I have often heard in the Dead of the Night (as I lay in Bed) echoing among the Mountains; he was kept by an English Gentleman at one of the Barracks, and it was loudly complained of by some of the Lairds, as being prejudicial to their Estates.

When a solemn Hunting is resolved on, for the entertainment of Relations and Friends, the Haunt of the Deer being known, a Number of the vassals are summoned, who readily obey by Inclination; and are, besides, obliged by the Tenure of their Lands, of which one Article is, that they shall attend the *Master* at his Huntings. This, I think, was Part of the ancient Vassalage in England.

The chief Convenes what Numbers he thinks fit, according to the Strength of his Clan : perhaps three or four hundred. With these he surrounds the Hill, and as they advance upwards, the Deer flies at the Sight of them, first of one Side, then of another; and they still, as they mount, get into closer Order, till, in the End, he is enclosed by them in a small Circle, and there they hack him down with their broad-Swords. And they generally do it so dexterously, as to preserve the Hide entire.

If the Chace be in a Wood, which is mostly upon the Declivity of a rocky Hill, the Tenants spread themselves as much as they can, in a Rank extending upwards; and march, or rather crawl forward, with a hideous Yell. Thus they drive every Thing before them, while the Laird and his Friends are waiting at the farther End with their Guns to shoot the Deer. But it is difficult to force the Roes out of their Cover; insomuch that when they come into the open Light, they sometimes turn back upon the Huntsmen, and are taken alive.

What I have been saying on this Head is only to give you some Taste of the Highland Hunting; for the Hills, as they are various in their Form, require different Dispositions of the Men that compose the Pack. The first of the two Paragraphs next above, relates only to such a Hill as rises something in the Figure of a Cone; and the other, you see, is the Side

of a Hill which is clothed with a Wood; and
this last is more particularly the Shelter of
the Roe. A further Detail I think would
become tedious.

When the Chief would have a Deer only
for his Household, the Game-Keeper and one
or two more are sent into the Hills with Guns,
and Oatmeal for their Provision, where they
often lie, Night after Night, to wait an Opportunity of providing Venison for the Family.
This has been done several Times for me, but
always without Effect.

The Foxes and wild Cats (or Cat·o'-
mountain) are both very large in their Kind,
and always appear to have fed plentifully;
they do the Highlanders much more hurt in
their Poultry, &c. than they yield them Profit
by their Furs; and the Eagles do them more
Mischief than both the others together. It
was one of their chief Complaints, when they
were disarmed, in the Year 1725, that they
were deprived of the Means to destroy those
noxious Animals, and that a great Increase of

them must necessarily follow the Want of their Fire-Arms.

Of the eatable Part of the feathered Kind peculiar to the Mountains is, First, the *Cobberkely*, which is sometimes called a wild Turkey, but not like it, otherwise than in Size. This is very seldom to be met with, being an Inhabitant of very high and unfrequented Hills, and is therefore esteemed a great Rarity for the Table. Next is the *black Cock*, which resembles, in Size and Shape, a Pheasant, but is black and shining, like a Raven; but the Hen is not, in Shape or Colour, much unlike to a Hen-Pheasant: and, lastly, the *Tormican*, near about the Size of the Moor-Fowl (or Grouse), but of a lighter Colour, which turns almost white in Winter. These, I am told, feed chiefly upon the tender Tops of the Fir-Branches, which I am apt to believe, because the Taste of them has something tending to Turpentine, though not disagreeable. It is said, if you throw a Stone so as to fall beyond it, the Bird is thereby so much amused or daunted, that it will not rise till you are very near; but I have suspected this to be a Sort of Conundrum, signifying they are too shy to suffer an Approach near enough for that Purpose, like what they tell the Children about the Salt and the Bird.

The Tribes will not suffer Strangers to settle within their Precinct, or even those of another Clan to enjoy any Possession among them; but will soon constrain them to quit their pretensions, by Cruelty to their Persons, or Mischief to their Cattle or other Property. Of this there happened two flagrant Instances, within a few Years past.

The first was as follows:—Gordon Laird of Glenbucket, had been invested by the D. of G. in some Lands in Badenoch, by Virtue, I think, of a *Wadset*, or Mortgage. These Lands lay among the Macphersons; but the Tenants of that Name refused to pay the Rent to the new Landlord, or to acknowledge him as such.

This Refusal put him upon the Means to

eject them by Law; whereupon the Tenants
came to a Resolution to put an End to his Suit
and new Settlement in the Manner following:
—Five or six of them, young Fellows, the
Sons of Gentlemen, entered the Door of his
Hut, and, in fawning Words, told him they
were sorry any Dispute had happened; that
they were then resolved to acknowledge him
as their immediate Landlord, and would
regularly pay him their Rent; at the same
Time they begged he would withdraw his
Process, and they hoped they should be agreeable to him for the future. All this while
they were almost imperceptibly drawing nearer
and nearer to his Bed-side, on which he was
sitting, in order to prevent his defending himself (as they knew him to be a Man of distinguished Courage), and then fell suddenly
on him, some cutting him with their Dirks,
and other plunging them into his Body. This
was perpetrated within Sight of the Banack of
Ruthven.

I cannot forbear to tell you how this

Butchery ended, with Respect both to him and those treacherous Villains. He, with a Multitude of Wounds upon him, made a Shift, in the Bustle, to reach down his broad-Sword from the Tester of his Bed, which was very low, and with it he drove all the Assassins before him; and afterwards, from the Duke's Abhorrence of so vile a Fact, and with the Assistance of the Troops, they were driven out of the Country, and forced to fly to foreign Parts.

By the Way, the Duke claims the Right of Chief to the Macphersons, as he is, in Fact, of the Gordons.

The other Example is of a Minister, who had a small Farm assigned him; and, upon his entrance to it, some of the Clan, in the Dead of the Night, fired five Balls through his Hut, which all lodged in his Bed; but he, happening to be absent that Night, escaped their Barbarity, but was forced to quit the Country. Of this he made to me an affecting Complaint.

This Kind of Cruelty, I think, arises from

their Dread of Innovations, and the Notion they entertain, that they have a Kind of hereditary Right to their Farms; and that none of them are to be dispossessed, unless for some great Transgression against their Chief, in which Case every Individual would consent to their Expulsion.

Having lately mentioned the Dirk, I think it may not be unseasonable here to give you a short Description of that dangerous Weapon; and the rather, as I may have Occasion to speak of it hereafter. The Blade is straight, and generally above a Foot long; the Back near [one-eighth of] an Inch thick; the Point goes off like a Tuck, and the Handle is something like that of a Sickle. They pretend they cannot do well without it, as being useful to them in cutting Wood, and upon many other Occasions; but it is a concealed Mischief, hid under the Plaid, ready for secret stabbing; and, in a close Encounter, there is no Defence against it.

I am far from thinking there is anything in

the Nature of a Highlander, as such, that
should make him cruel and remorseless; on
the contrary, I cannot but be of Opinion that
Nature in general is originally the same in all
Mankind, and that the Difference between
Country and Country arises from Education
and Example. And from this Principle I conclude, that even a Hottentot Child, being
brought into England before he had any
Knowledge, might, by a virtuous Education
and generous Example, become as much an
Englishman in his Heart as any Native whatever. But that the Highlanders, for the most
Part, are cruel, is beyond Dispute, though all
Clans are not alike merciless. In general
they have not Generosity enough to give
Quarter to an Enemy that falls in their Power;
nor do they seem to have any Remorse at shed-
ding Blood without Necessity.

This appeared a few Years ago, with
Respect to a Party of Soldiers, consisting
of a Serjeant and twelve Men, who were sent
into Lochaber after some Cows that were said

to be stolen. The Soldiers, with their Arms slung, were carelessly marching along by the Side of a Lake, where only one Man could pass in Front; and, in this Circumstance, fell into an Ambuscade of a great Number of Highlandmen, Vassals of an attainted Chief, who was in Exile when his Clan was accused of the Theft.

These were lodged in a Hollow on the Side of a rocky Hill; and though they were themselves out of all Danger, or might have descended and disarmed so small a Party, yet they chose rather, with their Fire-Arms, as it were wantonly to pick them off, almost one by one, till they had destroyed them all, except two, who took to their Heels, and waded a small River into the Territory of another Chief, where they were safe from further Pursuit; for the Chiefs, like Princes upon the Continent whose Dominions lie contiguous, do not invade each other's Boundaries while they are in Peace and Friendship with one another, but demand Redress of Wrongs; and

whosoever should do otherwise, would commit
an Offence in which every Tribe is interested,
besides the lasting Feud it might create between
the two neighbouring Clans.

P. S. One of these Soldiers, who, in his
Flight, had fixed his Bayonet, turned about at
the Edge of the Water upon a Highlandman,
who, for greater Speed, had no other Arms
than his broad-Sword, and, at the same Time,
it is said, the Soldier at once sent his Bayonet
and a Ball through his Body.

LETTER XXII.

BUT the Rancour of some of those People, in another Case, was yet more extraordinary than the Instance in my last letter, as the Objects of their Malice could not seem, even to the utmost Cowardice, to be in any Manner of Condition to annoy them. This was after the Battle of Glenshiels, in the Rebellion of 1719, before-mentioned. As the Troops were marching from the Field of Action to a Place of Encampment, some of the Men who were dangerously wounded, after their being carried some little Way on Horseback, complained they could no longer bear that uneasy Carriage, and begged they might be left behind till some more gentle Conveyance could be provided.

In about three or four Hours (the little Army being encamped) Parties were sent to them with Hurdles, that had been made to serve as a Kind of Litters; but, when they arrived, they found to their Astonishment that those poor, miserable Creatures had been stabbed with Dirks in twenty Places of their Legs and Arms, as well as their Bodies, and even those that were dead had been used in the same savage Manner. This I have been assured of by several Officers who were in the Battle, Scots as well as English.

I make no manner of Doubt you will take what is to follow to be an odd Transition, *i. e.* from the Cruelty of the ordinary Highlanders, to Dialect and Orthography,—although you have met with some others not more consistent; but then you will recollect what I said in my first Epistle, that I should not confine myself to Method, but give you my account just as the several Parts of the Subject should occur from my Memorandums and Memory.

Strange Encomiums I have heard from the Natives upon the Language of their Country, although it be but a Corruption of the Irish

Tongue; and, if you could believe some of them, it is so expressive, that it wants only to be better known to become universal. But as for myself, who can only judge of it by the Ear, it seems to me to be very harsh in Sound, like the Welsh, and altogether as gutteral, which last, you know, is a Quality long since banished all the polite Languages in Europe.

It likewise seems to me, as if the Natives affected to call it Erst, as though it were a Language peculiar to their Country; but an Irish Gentleman who never before was in Scotland, and made with me a Highland Tour, was perfectly understood even by the common People; and several of the Lairds took me aside to ask me who he was, for that they never heard their Language spoken in such Purity before. This Gentleman told me that he found the Dialect to vary as much in different Parts of the Country as in any two Counties of England. There are very few who can write the Character, of which the Alphabet is as follows:—

Pronounced

a	𝔄	*a*	Ailim.
b	*b*	*b*	Beith.
c	C	*c*	Coll.
d	ᶀ	ᶁ	Duir.
e	*e*	*e*	Eadha.
f	F	ꝼ	Fearn.
g	Ʒ	ᵹ	Gort.
h	𝔎	ħ	Uath.
j i	ꟻ ∫	ᶈ '	Jogha.
l	ℓ	ℓ	Luis.
m	𝔐	*m*	Muin.
n	N	*n*	Nuin.
o	O	o	Oun.
p	P	p	Peithboc.
r	R	ᴎ	Ruïs.
s	S	ſ	Suil.
t	C	ᴢ	Tinne.
u	U	*u*	Uir.

In writing English, they seem to have no Rule of Orthography, and they profess they think good Spelling of no great use; but if

T. Jefferys sculp

they read English Authors, I wonder their
Memory does not retain the Figures, or Forms
of common Words, especially Monosyllables;
but it may, for aught I know, be Affectation.

I have frequently received Letters from Ministers and lay Gentlemen, both esteemed for
their Learning in dead Languages, that have
been so ill Spelt, I thought I might have expected better from an ordinary Woman in
England. As for one single example, for
Heirs (of Latin Derivation,) *Airs* repeated
several times in the same Letter; and, further,
one Word was often variously spelt in the same
Page.

The Highland Dress consists of a Bonnet
made of Thrum without a Brim, a short Coat,
a Waistcoat, longer by five or six Inches, short
Stockings, and Brogues, or· Pumps without
Heels. By the way, they cut Holes in their
Brogues, though new made, to let out the
Water, when they have far to go and Rivers
to pass: this they do to preserve their Feet
from galling.

Few besides Gentlemen wear the *Trowze*,— that is, the Breeches and Stockings all of one piece, and drawn on together; over this Habit they wear a Plaid, which is usually three Yards long and two Breadths wide, and the whole Garb is made of chequered Tartan, or Plaiding: this, with the Sword and Pistol, is called a *full Dress*, and, to a well-proportioned Man, with any tolerable Air, it makes an agreeable Figure; but this you have seen in London, and it is chiefly their Mode of dressing when they are in the Lowlands, or when they make a neighbouring Visit, or go any-where on Horseback; but when those among them who travel on Foot, and have not attend-ants to carry them over the Waters, they vary it into the *Quelt*, which is a Manner I am about to describe.

The common Habit of the ordinary High-landers is far from being acceptable to the Eye; with them a small Part of the Plaid, which is not so large as the former, is set in Folds and girt round the Waist, to make of it

a short Petticoat that reaches half way down
the Thigh, and the rest is brought over the
Shoulders, and then fastened before, below the
Neck, often with a Fork, and sometimes with
a Bodkin, or sharpened Piece of Stick, so that
they make pretty nearly the Appearance of the
poor Women in London when they bring their
Gowns over their Heads to shelter them from
the Rain.　In this way of wearing the Plaid,
they have sometimes nothing else to cover
them, and are often barefoot ; but some I
have seen shod with a kind of Pumps, made
out of a raw Cow-hide, with the Hair turned
outward, which being ill-made, the Wearer's
Foot looked something like those of a rough-
Footed Hen or Pigeon : these are called
Quarrants, and are not only offensive to the
Sight but intolerable to the Smell of those
who are near them.　The Stocking rises no
higher than the Thick of the Calf, and from
the Middle of the thigh to the middle of the
Leg is a naked space, which being exposed to
all Weathers, becomes tanned and freckled,

and the Joint being mostly infected with the
Country Distemper, the whole is very disagreeable to the Eye. This Dress is called
the *Quelt ;* and, for the most part they wear
the Petticoat so very short, that in a windy
Day, going up a Hill, or stooping, the In-
decency of it is plainly discovered.

A Highland Gentleman told me one Day
merrily, as we were speaking of a dangerous
Precipice we had passed over together, that a
Lady of a noble Family had complained to
him very seriously, that as she was going over
the same Place with a *Gilly,* who was upon
an upper Path leading her Horse with a long
String, she was so terrified with the Sight of
the Abyss, that, to avoid it, she was forced to
look up towards the bare Highlander all the
Way long.

I have observed before, that the Plaid serves
the ordinary People for a Cloak by Day and
Bedding at Night : By the latter it imbibes
so much Perspiration, that no one Day can
free it from the filthy Smell ; and even some of

better than ordinary Appearance, when the Plaid falls from the shoulder, or otherwise requires to be re-adjusted, while you are talking with them, toss it over again, as some People do the Knots of their Wigs, which conveys the Offence in Whiffs that are intolerable;—of this they seem not to be sensible, for it is often done only to give themselves Airs.

Various Reasons are given both for and against the Highland Dress. It is urged against it, that it distinguishes the Natives as a Body of People distinct and separate from the rest of the Subjects of Great Britian, and thereby is one Cause of their narrow Adherence among themselves, to the Exclusion of all the rest of the Kingdom ; but the Part of the Habit chiefly objected to is the Plaid (or Mantle), which they say, is calculated for the Encouragement of an idle Life in lying about upon the Heath, in the Day-time, instead of following some lawful Employment; that it serves to cover them in the Night when they lie in wait among the Mountains, to commit their Robberies and Depredations; and is composed of such Colours as altogether, in the Mass, so nearly resemble the Heath on which they lie, that it is hardly to be distinguished from it until one is so near them as to be within their Power, if they have any evil Intention; that it renders them ready at a Moment's Warning, to join in any Rebellion, as they carry continually their Tents about them; and lastly, it was thought necessary, in Ireland, to suppress that Habit by Act of Parliament, for the above Reasons, and no Complaint for the want of it now remains among the Mountaineers of that Country.

On the other hand, it is alleged, the Dress is most convenient to those who, with no ill Design are obliged to travel from one Part to another upon their lawful Occasions, viz.—That they would not be so free to skip over the Rocks and Bogs with breeches as they are in the short Petticoat; that it would be greatly incommodious to those who are frequently to

wade through Waters, to wear Breeches, which
must be taken off upon every such Occurrence,
or would not only gall the Wearer, but render
it very unhealthful and dangerous to their
Limbs, to be constantly wet in that Part of
the Body, especially in Winter-time, when
they might be frozen: and with respect to
the Plaid in particular, the Distance between
one Place of Shelter and another, is often too
great to be reached before Night comes on;
and, being intercepted by sudden Floods, or
hindered by other Impediments, they are frequently obliged to lie all Night in the Hills, in
which Case they must perish, were it not for
the Covering they carry with them. That
even if they should be so fortunate as to reach
some hospitable Hut, they must lie upon the
Ground uncovered, there being nothing to be
spared from the Family for that Purpose.

And to conclude, a few Shillings will buy
this Dress for an ordinary Highlander, who,
very probably, might hardly ever be in Condition to purchase a Lowland Suit, though of

the coarsest Cloth or Stuff, fit to keep him warm in that cold Climate.

I shall determine nothing in this Dispute, but leave you to judge which of these two Reasonings is the most cogent.

The whole People are fond and tenacious of the Highland Clothing, as you may believe by what is here to follow.

Being, in a wet Season, upon one of my Peregrinations, accompanied by a Highland Gentleman, who was one of the Clan through which I was passing, I observed the Woman to be in great anger with him about something that I did not understand: at length, I asked him wherein he had offended them? Upon this Question he laughed, and told me his great-Coat was the Cause of their Wrath; and that their Reproach was, that he could not be contented with the Garb of his Ancestors, but was degenerated into a Lowlander, and condescended to follow their unmanly Fashions.

The wretched Appearance of the poor Highland Women that come to this Town, has been mentioned; and here I shall step out of the way to give you a notable Instance of Frugality in one of a higher Rank.

There is a Laird's Lady, about a Mile from one of the Highland Garrisons, who is often seen from the Ramparts, on Sunday Mornings, coming barefoot to the Kirk, with her Maid carrying the Stockings and Shoes after her. She Stops at the Foot of a certain Rock, that serves her for a Seat, not far from the Hovel they call a Church, and there she puts them on; and, in her Return to the same Place, she prepares to go home barefoot as she came; thus, reversing the old Mosaic Precept. What English Squire was ever blessed with such a Housewife!

But this Instance, though true to my Knowledge, I have thought something extraordinary, because the Highlanders are shy of exposing their Condition to Strangers, especially the English, and more particularly to a Number of Officers, to whom they are generally desirous to make their best Appearance. But, in my Journeys, when they did not expect to be observed by any but their own Country People, I have twice surprised the Laird and his Lady without Shoes or Stockings, a good Way from Home, in cold Weather. The Kirk abovementioned brings to my Memory a Curiosity of the same kind.

At a Place in Badenoch, called Ilan Dou, as I passed by a Hut of Turf something larger than ordinary, but taking little notice of it, I was called upon by one of the Company to stop and observe its Figure, which proved to be the Form of a Cross: this occasioned several Jokes from a Libertine and a Presbyterian upon the Highland Cathedral and the Non-Jurors, in all which they perfectly agreed.

The ordinary Girls wear nothing upon their Heads until they are married or have a Child, except sometimes a Fillet of red or blue coarse Cloth, of which they are very proud; but often their hair hangs down over the Forehead like that of a wild Colt.

If they wear Stockings, which is very rare,
they lay them in Plaits one above another, from
the Ancle up to the Calf, to make their Legs
appear as near as they can in the Form of a
Cylinder; but I think I have seen something
like this among the poor German Refugee
Women and the Moorish Men in London.
By the way, these Girls, if they have no
Pretensions to Family (as many of them have,
though in Rags), they are vain of being with
Child by a Gentleman ; and when he makes
Love to one of them, she will plead her excuse,
in saying he undervalues himself, and that she
is a poor Girl not worth his Trouble, or something to that Purpose.

This easy Compliance proceeds chiefly from
a kind of Ambition established by Opinion and
Custom; for as Gentility is of all things
esteemed the most valuable in the Notion of
those People, so this kind of Commerce
renders the poor plebeian Girl, in some
Measure, superior to her former Equals.

From thenceforward she becomes proud,

and they grow envious of her being singled
out from among them, to receive the Honour
of a Gentleman's particular Notice : but otherwise they are generally far from being im-
modest ; and as Modesty is the Capital
feminine Virtue, in that they may be a Reproach to some in higher Circumstances, who
have lost that decent and endearing Quality.

You know I should not venture to talk in
this manner at———, where Modesty would
be decried as impolite and troublesome, and I
and my slender Party ridiculed and borne
down by a vast Majority. I shall here give
you a Sample of the Wretchedness of some of
them.

In one of my northern Journeys, where I
travelled in a good deal of Company, there
was, among the rest, a Scots Baronet, who is
a Captain in the Army, and does not seem (at
least to me) to affect Concealment of his
Country's Disadvantage. This Gentleman, at
our Inn, when none but he and I were together, examined the Maid-servant about her

way of living; and she told him (as he interpreted it to me) that she never was in a Bed
in her Life, or ever took off her Clothes while
they would hang together: but in this last, I
think, she was too general; for I am pretty
sure she was forced to pull them off now and
then for her own Quiet. But I must go a
little further.

One Half of the Hut, by Partition, was
taken up with the Field-bed of the principal
Person among us, and therefore the Man and
his Wife very courteously offered to sit up and
leave their Bed to the Baronet and me (for the
rest of the Company were dispersed about in
Barns); but we could not resolve to accept the
Favour, for certain Reasons, but chose rather
to lie upon the Benches with our Saddles for
Pillows.

Being in a high Part of the Country, the
Night was excessive cold, with some Snow
upon the mountains, though in August, and
the next Day was the hottest I think I
ever felt in my Life.

The violent Heat of the Sun among the Rocks, made my new Companions (Natives of the Hovel) such voracious Cannibals that I was obliged to lag behind, and set my Servant to take Vengeance on them for the plentiful Repast they were making at my Expense, and without my Consent, and by which I was told they were become as red as Blood. But I should have let you know, that when the Table over-Night was spread with such Provisions as were carried with us, our chief Man would needs have the Lady of the House to grace the Board; and it fell to my Lot to sit next to her till I had loaded her Plate, and bid her go and sup with her Husband, for I fore-saw the Consequence of our Conjunction.

The young Children of the ordinary Highlanders are miserable Objects indeed, and are mostly over-run with that Distemper which some of the old Men are hardly ever freed of from their Infancy. I have often seen them come out from the Huts early in a cold Morning stark naked, and squat themselves down (if I might decently use the Comparison) like Dogs on a Dunghill, upon a certain Occasion after confinement. And at other Times they have but little to defend them from the Inclemencies of the Weather in so cold a Climate: nor are the Children of some Gentlemen in much better Condition, being strangely neglected till they are six or seven Years old: this one might know by a Saying I have often heard, viz.—"That a Gentleman's Bearns are to be distinguished by their speaking English."

I was invited one Day to dine with a Laird, not very far within the Hills; and, observing about the House, an English Soldier, whom I had often seen before in this Town, I took an opportunity to ask him several Questions.

This Man was a Bird-Catcher, and employed by the Laird to provide him with small Birds, for the Exercise of his Hawks. Among other things, he told me that for three or four Days after his first coming, he had observed in the Kitchen (an Out-house Hovel) a Parcel of dirty Children half naked, whom he took to belong to some poor Tenant, till at last he found they were a Part of the Family; but, although these were so little regarded, the young Laird, about the Age of fourteen, was going to the University; and the eldest Daughter, about sixteen, sat with us at Table, clean and genteelly dressed.

But, perhaps, it may seem, that in this and other Observations of the like kind, whenever I have met with one particular Fact, I would make it thought to be general. I do assure you it is not so: but when I have known any thing to be common, I have endeavoured to illustrate it by some particular Example. Indeed, there is hardly any Thing of this sort that I have mentioned, can be so general as to be free from all Exception; it is Justification enough to me if the Matter be generally known to answer my Description, or what I have related of it. But I think an Apology of this Nature to you is needless. It is impossible for me, from my own Knowledge, to give you an

Account of the ordinary Way of Living of those Gentlemen; because, when any of us (the English) are invited to their Houses, there is always an Appearance of Plenty to Excess; and it has been often said they will ransack all their Tenants rather than we should think meanly of their Housekeeping: but I have heard it from many whom they have employed, and perhaps had little regard to their Observations as inferior People, that, although they have been attended at Dinner by five or six Servants, yet, with all that State, they have often dined upon Oatmeal varied several ways, pickled Herrings, or other such cheap and indifferent Diet: but though I could not personally know their ordinary Bill of Fare, yet I have had Occasion to observe they do not live in the cleanest manner, though some of them, when in England, affect the utmost Nicety in that Particular.

A Friend of mine told me, some time ago, that, in his Journey hither, he stopped to bait at the Bull Inn, at Stamford, which, I think,

is one among the best in England. He soon
received a Message by the Landlord, from two
Gentlemen in the next Room, who were going
from these Parts to London, proposing they
might all dine together: this he readily consented to, as being more agreeable to him than
dining alone.

As they sat at Table, waiting for Dinner,
one of them found fault with the Table-cloth,
and said it was not clean; there was, it seems,
a Spot or two upon it, which he told them
was only the Stain of Claret, that could not at
once be perfectly washed out; then they wiped
their Knives, Forks, and Plates with the Nap-
kins; and, in short, nothing was clean enough
for them;—and this to a Gentleman who is
himself extremely nice in every Thing of that
Nature. At last, says my Friend, vexed at
the impertinent Farce, as he called it, " Gentlemen, I am vastly pleased at your Dislikes, as
I am now upon my Journey to Scotland (where
I have never yet been), because I must infer
I shall there find these Things in better Con-

dition." "Troth," says one of them, "ye canno want it."

I am sorry for such Instances, whereby a Fop, conscious of the Fallacy, exposes his Country, and brings a Ridicule upon other Gentlemen of Modesty and good Sense, to serve a momentary Vanity, if not to give Affronts, by such gross Impositions.

I know very well what my Friend thinks of them now, and, perhaps, by their Means, of many others who do not deserve it.

There is one Gasconade of the People hereabouts, which is extraordinary : they are often boasting of the great Hospitality of the Highlanders to Strangers ; for my own Part, I do not remember to have received one Invitation from them, but when it was with an apparent View to their own Interest : on the contrary, I have several times been unasked to eat, though there was nothing to be purchased within many Miles of the Place. But one particular Instance was most inhospitable. Being benighted, soon after it was dark, I

made up to the House of one to whom I was
well known ; and, though I had five or six Miles
to travel over a dangerous rugged Way, wherein there was no other Shelter to be expected ;
yet, upon the Trampling of my Horses before
the House, the Lights went out in the Twink-
ling of an Eye, and Deafness at once seized
the whole Family.

The latter Part of what I have written of
this Letter relates chiefly to Gentlemen who
inhabit the Hills not far from the Borders of
the Lowlands, or not very far from the Sea, or
Communication with it by Lakes ; as, indeed,
most Part of the Houses of the Chiefs of
Clans are in one or other of these Situations.
These are sometimes built with Stone and
Lime, and though not large, except some few,
are pretty commodious, at least with Comparison to these that are built in the manner
of the Huts, of which, if any one has a Room
above, it is, by way of Eminence, called a
lofted House ; but in the inner Part of the
Mountains there are no Stone Buildings that

I know of, except the Barracks; and one may go a hundred Miles an-end without seeing any other Dwellings than the common Huts of Turf.

I have, indeed, heard of one that was intended to be built with Stone in a remote Part of the Highlands, from whence the Laird sent a number of Highlanders with Horses to fetch a Quantity of Lime from the Borders; but, in their way Home, there happened to fall a good deal of Rain, and the Lime began to crackle and smoke. The Highlanders not thinking, of all Things, Water would occasion Fire, threw it all into a shallow Rivulet, in order to quench it before they proceeded further homeward; and this, they say, put an End to the Project. But I take this to be a Lowland Sneer upon the Highlanders, though not improbable.

I have mentioned above, among other situations of Stone-Built Houses, some that are near to Lakes which have a Communication with the Sea.

There are, in several Parts of the Highlands, winding Hollows between the Feet of the Mountains whereinto the Sea flows, of which Hollows some are navigable for Ships of Burden, for ten or twenty Miles together inland : those the Natives call *Lochs*, or Lakes, although they are salt, and have a Flux and Reflux, and therefore, more properly, should be called Arms of the Sea. I could not but think this Explanation necessary, to distinguish those Waters from the standing fresh-water Lakes, which I have endeavoured to describe in a former Letter.

LETTER XXIII.

WHEN a young Couple are married, for
the First Night the Company keep
Possession of the Dwelling-House or Hut, and
send the Bridegroom and Bride to a Barn or
Out-House, giving them Straw, Heath, or
Fern, for a Bed, with Blankets for their
covering; and then they make Merry, and
dance to the Piper all the Night long.

Soon after the Wedding-Day, the new-
married Woman sets herself about spinning
her winding-Sheet, and a Husband that should
sell or pawn it, is esteemed, among all Men,
one of the most profligate.

At a young Highlander's first setting up for
himself, if he be of any Consideration, he goes
about among his near Relations and Friends;
and from one he begs a Cow, from another a
Sheep; a third gives him Seed to sow his

Land, and so on, till he has procured for himself a tolerable Stock for a Beginner. This they call *Thigging*.

After the Death of any one, not in the lowest Circumstances, the Friends and Acquaintance of the Deceased assemble to keep the near Relations Company the first Night; and they dance, as if it were at a Wedding, till the next Morning, though all the Time the Corpse lies before them in the same Room. If the deceased be a Woman, the Widower leads up the first Dance; if a Man the Widow. But this Highland Custom I knew to my Disturbance, within less than a Quarter of a Mile of Edinburgh, before I had been among the Mountains. It was upon the Death of a Smith, next Door to my Lodgings, who was a Highlander.

The upper Class hire Women to moan and lament at the Funeral of their nearest Relations. These Women cover their Heads with a small Piece of Cloth, mostly green, and every now and then break out into a hideous Howl and Ho-bo-bo-bo-boo, as I have often heard is done in some Parts of Ireland.

This Part of the Ceremony is called a *Coronoch*, and, generally speaking, is the Cause of much Drunkenness, attended with its Concomitants, mischievous Rencounters and bloody Broils ; for all that have Arms in their Possession, accoutre themselves with them upon those Occasions.

I have made Mention of their Funeral-Piles in a former Letter ; but I had once Occasion to take particular Notice of a Heap of Stones, near the Middle of a small Piece of Arable Land. The Plough was carefully guided as near to it as possible ; and the Pile, being like others I had seen upon the Moors, I asked, by an Interpreter, whether there was a Rock beneath it ; but being answered in the Negative, I further inquired the Reasons why they lost so much Ground, and did not Remove the Heap. To this I had for Answer, it was a Burial Place, and they deemed it a Kind of Sacrilege to remove a single Stone ; and that the Child-

II   O

ren, from their infancy, were taught the same
Veneration for it. Thus a Parcel of loose
Stones are more religiously preserved among
them than, with us, the costly Monuments in
Westminster-Abbey ; and thence I could not
but conclude that the Inclination to preserve
the Remains and Memory of the Dead is
greater with those People than it is among us.
The Highlanders, even here in this Town,
cannot forego the Practice of the Hills, in
raising Heaps of Stones over such as have lost
their Lives by some Misfortune; for in Oliver's
Fort, no sooner was the Body of an Officer
removed from the Place where he fell in a
Duel, than they set about the raising such a
Heap of Stones upon the Spot where he had
lain.   So much for Mountain Monuments.

Those who are said to have the *second
Sight* deal chiefly in Deaths, and it is often
said to be a Gift peculiar to some Families ;—
that is, the Cheat has, with some, been handed
down from Father to Son ; yet I must confess
they seldom fail to be right when they reveal

their Predictions, for they take the surest Method to prophetise, which is to divulge the Oracle after the Fact. Of this I had once an Opportunity to convince a Highland Gentleman, from whom I thought might have been expected more Reason and less Prejudice, than to be gulled by such Impostors.

The Matter was this :—A poor Highlander was drowned in wading a Ford, and his Body afterwards put into a small Barn ; not many Days after, the Laird endeavouring to pass the same Water, which was hard by his own House, his Horse gave Way, and he was likewise drowned, and carried into the same Hut. Soon after, a Story began to pass for current, that such-a-one, the *second-sighted*, foretold, when the Body of the poor Man lay exposed to View, that it would not be long before a greater Man than he should lie in the same Place. This was all that was pretended, and that too was afterwards found to be an Invention, arising from the Circumstance of two Persons at a little Distance of Time, being

drowned in the same Ford, and both their
Bodies carried to one Hovel, which, indeed,
stood singly, near the Place where they were
both stopped by the Rocks.

Witches and Goblins are likewise pretty
common among the Highlanders, and they
have several old Prophecies handed down to
them by Tradition ; among which, this is one,
That the Time shall come when they shall
measure out the Cloth of London with a long
Pole.

As the little Manufacture they had was
Cloth, so, at the Time when this pretended
Prophecy was broached, they esteemed that
the only Riches, and did not know of the
Treasure of Lombard-Street ; like the Country
Boy, that fed poorly and worked hard, who
said, if he were a Gentleman, he would eat fat
Bacon, and swing all Day long upon Gaffer
Such-a-one's *Yate*.

A certain Laird, whom I have mentioned
several Times before, though not by Name, is
frequently heard to affirm, that, at the Instant

he was born, a Number of Swords, that hung
up in the Hall of the Mansion-House, leaped
of themselves out of the Scabbards, in Token,
I suppose, that he was to be a mighty Man in
Arms; and this vain Romance seems to be
believed by the lower Order of his Followers;
and I believe there are many that laugh at it
in Secret, who dare not publicly declare their
Disbelief. But, because the Miracle has
hitherto only portended the Command of his
Clan and an independent Company, he has
endeavoured to supply the Defeat of the
Presage by his own Epitaph, altogether as
romantic, in his own Kirk, which he still lives
to read, whenever he pleases to gratify his
Vanity with the Sight of it.

They have an odd Notion relating to dead
Bodies that are to be transported over Rivers,
Lakes, or Arms of the Sea: before it is put
on Board they appraise and ascertain the Value
of the Boat or Vessel, believing, if that be
neglected, some Accident will happen to
endanger the Lives of those who are embarked

in it; but, upon Recollection, I think some of our Seamen entertain this idle Fancy in some Measure; for, I have heard, they do not care for a Voyage with a Corpse on Board, as though it would be the Occasion of tempestuous Weather; and, lastly (for I shall not trouble you longer with Things of this Kind, which are without Number), the Highlanders are of Opinion, that it is in the Power of certain Enchantresses to prevent the Act of Procreation; but I am rather inclined to believe it was originally a Male Artifice among them to serve as an Excuse in case of Imbecility.

The Marriages of the Chiefs and Chieftains are, for the most Part, confined to the Circuit of the Highlands; and they generally endeavour to strengthen their Clan by what they call powerful Alliances: but I must not be understood to include any of the prime Nobility of Scotland, of whom there are some Chiefs of Clans: their Dignity places them quite out of the Reach of any Thing I have said, or have to say, in relation to the Heads of Highland Families, who reside constantly with them, and govern them in Person. As to the lower Class of Gentry and the ordinary People, they generally marry in the Clan whereto they appertain.

All this may be political enough, *i. e.*, the Chief to have Regard to the Highlands in general, and his Followers to their own particular Tribe or Family, in order to preserve themselves a distinct People; but this continues them in a narrow Way of thinking with Respect to the rest of Mankind and also prevents that Addition to the Circumstances of the whole, or Part of the Highlands, which might be made by Marriages of Women of Fortune in the Lowlands. This, in Time, might have a good Effect, by producing an Union, instead of that Coldness, to say no more, which subsists, at present, between the Natives of those two Parts of Scotland, as if they bore no relation one to another, considered as Men and Subjects of the same Kingdom,

and even the same Part of it. Yet I must
here (and by the bye) take Notice of one
Thing, wherein they perfectly agree, which
Experience has taught me to know perfectly
well; and that is, to grudge and envy those of
the South Part of the Island any profitable
Employment among them, although they themselves are well received and equally encouraged
and employed with the Natives in that Part of
the Kingdom; and I think further, they have
sometimes more than their Share, if they must
needs keep up such a partial and invidious
Distinction.

But to return to the Marriages of the Highlanders,——Perhaps, after what has been said of
the Country, it may be asked, what Lowland
Woman would care to lead a Life attended with
so many Inconveniences? Doubtless there
are those who would be as fond of sharing the
clanish State and Power with a Husband, as
some others are of a Name, when they sell
themselves for a Title; for each of these
Kinds of Vanity is very flattering: besides,

there are many of the Lowland Women who seem to have a great liking to the Highland-men, which they cannot forbear to insinuate in their ordinary Conversation. But such Marriages are very rare; and I know but one Instance of them, which, I must confess, will not much recommend the Union of which I have been speaking; but then it is but one, and cannot be the Cause of any general In-ference.

A certain Chieftain took to Wife the Daughter of an Edinburgh Goldsmith; but this Lowland Match was the Cause of much Discontent in the Tribe, as being not only a Diminution of the Honour of the House, but, in their Opinion, an ill Precedent besides; and nothing was more common among the People of that Branch of the Clan, than to ask among themselves—" Were there not Smiths enough in the Clan that had Daughters? How comes our Chief then to have married the Daughter of a Lowland Smith?" Making no Distinction between an Edinburgh Goldsmith and a Highland Blacksmith. They thought it was a Disgrace, of which every one partook, that he should match himself with a Tradesman's Daughter, a Lowland Woman, and no Way derived from the Tribe.

This proved in the End to be a fatal Marriage; but as it is uncertain, and therefore would be unjust for me to determine, in a Matter whereof I have not a perfect knowledge, I cannot conclude which of the two, the Husband or the Wife, was the Occasion of the sad Catastrophe. I shall only say what I know, viz. that an old rough Highlander, of sixty at least, was imprisoned at one of the Barracks, while I was there, for accepting Favours from the Lady. She was to be sent to Edinburgh to answer the Accusation; and, while she was preparing to go, and the Messenger waiting without Doors, to conduct her thither—*she died*.

The Clan whereto the above mentioned Tribe belongs, is the only one I have heard of which is without a Chief;—that is, being

divided into Families under several Chieftains,
without any particular Patriarch of the whole
Name : and this is a great Reproach, as may
appear from an Affair that fell out at my
Table in the Highlands, between one of that
Name and a Cameron. The Provocation
given by the latter was *Name your Chief.*—
The return to it at once was, *You are a Fool.*
They went out the next Morning ; but, having
early Notice of it, I sent a small Party of
Soldiers after them, which, in all Probability,
prevented some barbarous Mischief that might
have ensued ; for the Chiefless Highlander,
who is himself a petty Chieftain, was going to
the Place appointed with a small-Sword and
Pistol, whereas the Cameron (an old Man)
took with him only his Broad-Sword, according
to Agreement.

When all was over, and I had at least seemingly reconciled them, I was told the Words
(of which I seem to think but slightly), were
to one of that Clan the greatest of all Provocations.

In a Bargain between two Highlanders, each of them wets the Ball of his Thumb with his Mouth, and then joining them together, it is esteemed a very binding Act; but in more solemn Engagements, they take an Oath in a Manner which I shall describe in some succeeding Letter.

When any one of them is armed at all Points, he is loaded with a Target, a Firelock, a heavy Broad-Sword, a Pistol, Stock and Lock of Iron, a Dirk; and, besides all these, some of them carry a Sort of Knife, which they call a *Skeen-ochles*, from its being concealed in the Sleeve near the Arm-pit.

This last is more peculiar to the Robbers, who have done Mischief with it, when they were thought to have been effectually disarmed.

To see a Highlander thus furnished out might put one in mind of *Merry Andrew*, when he comes from behind the Curtain, in a warlike Manner, to dispute the Doctor's Right to his Stage.   He is then, in his own individual

Person, a whole Company of Foot, being
loaded with one of every Species of the Arms
and Trophies of a Regiment, viz. a Pike,
Halbert, Firelock, Sword, Bayonet, Colours,
and Drum.

Sometimes, when a Company of them have
previously resolved and agreed to be peaceable
and friendly over their Usky, they have drawn
their Dirks and stuck them all into the
[*Cheese*] Table before them, as who should
say, " Nothing but peace at this Meeting—no
private stabbing to night." But, in promis-
cuous Companies, at great Assemblies, such
as Fairs, Burials, &c., where much Drunkenness
prevails, there scarcely ever fails to be great
Riots and much Mischief done among them.

To shoot at a Mark, they lay themselves all
along behind some Stone or Hillock on which
they rest their Piece, and are a long while
taking their Aim ; by which Means they can
destroy any one unseen, on whom they would
wreak their Malice or Revenge.

When in Sight of the Enemy, they endeavour to possess themselves of the higher Ground, as knowing they give their Fire more effectually by their Situation one above another, being without Discipline; and also that they afterwards descend on the Enemy with greater Force, having in some Measure, put it out of their Power to recede in the first Onset.

After their first Fire (I need not have said their first, for they rarely stand a second), they throw away their Fire-Arms and Plaids which encumber them, and make their Attack with their Swords; but if repulsed, they seldom or never rally, but return to their Habitations. If they happen to engage in a Plain, when they expect the Enemy's Fire, they throw themselves down on the Ground. They had ever a Dread of the Cavalry, and did not care to engage them, though but few in Number.

I chanced to be in Company one Time with an old Highlander, as I passed over the Plain of Killicranky, where the Battle was fought between King William's Troops, commanded by

General Mackay, and the Rebel Highlanders under the Earl [*Viscount*] of Dundee.

When he came to the great Stone that is raised about the Middle of the flat, upon the Spot where Dundee fell, we stopped; and there he described to me, in his Manner, the Order and End of the Battle, of which I shall now give you the Substance only, for he was long in telling his Story.

He told me that Mackay extended his Line, which was only two deep, the whole Length of the Plain; designing, as he supposed, to surround the Highlanders, if they should descend from the Side of an opposite Hill, where they were posted. That after the first Firing, the Rebels came down, six or seven deep, to attack the King's Troops; and their Rear pushing on their Front, they by their Weight charged through and through these Feeble Files; and, having broke them, made with their Broad-Swords a most cruel Carnage; and many others who expected no Quarter, in order to escape the Highland Fury, threw themselves into that rapid River (the Tay), and were drowned. But he said there was an English Regiment who kept themselves entire (the only one that was there), whom the Highlanders did not care to attack; and, after the Slaughter was over and the Enemy retired, that single Corps marched from the Field in good Order. He further told me, there were some few Horse badly mounted, who, by the strength of the Highland Files were pushed into the River, which was close in their Rear.

On any sudden Alarm and Danger or Distress to the Chief, he gives notice of it throughout his own Clan, and to such others as are in Alliance with him. This is done by sending a Signal, which they call the *Fiery-Cross*, being two Sticks tied together transversely, and burnt at the Ends; with this, he sends Directions in Writing, to signify the Place of Rendezvous. And when the principal Person of any Place has received this Token, he dismisses the Messenger, and sends it forward to another; and so on, till all have received the Intelligence. Upon the Receipt of this Signal, all that are near immediately leave Habitations, and repair to the Place appointed, with their Arms, and Oatmeal for their Provision. This they mingle with the Water of the next River or Bourn they come to when Hunger calls for a Supply; and often, for Want of a proper Vessel, sup the raw Mixture out of the Palms of their Hands.

They have been used to impose a Tax upon the Inhabitants of the Low-Country, near the Borders of the Highlands, called *Black Mail* (or Rent), and levy it upon them by Force; and sometimes upon the weaker Clans among themselves. But as it was made equally criminal, by several Acts of Parliament, to comply with this Exaction and to extort it, the People, to avoid the Penalty, came to Agreement with the Robbers, or some of their Correspondents in the Lowlands, to protect their Houses and Cattle. And, as long as this Payment was punctually made, the Depreda-

II.   P

tions ceased, or otherwise the Collector of this Imposition was by Contract obliged to make good the Loss, which he seldom failed to do.

These Collectors gave regular Receipts, as for Safeguard Money; and those who refused to pay it, were sure to be plundered, except they kept a continual Guard of their own, well armed, which would have been a yet more expensive Way of securing their Property. And, notwithstanding the Guard of the independent Highland Companies, which were raised chiefly to prevent Thefts and Impositions of this Nature, yet I have been certainly informed, that this *Black Mail*, or evasive Safeguard-Money, has been very lately paid in a disarmed Part of the northern Highlands; and, I make no doubt, in other Places besides, though it has not yet come to my Knowledge.

The gathering-in of Rents is called *uplifting* them, and the stealing of Cows they call *Lifting*, a softening Word for Theft; as if it were only collecting their Dues. This I have often heard; but it has so often occurred to me, that we have the Word *Shop-lifting*, in the Sense of stealing, which I take to be an old English compound Word. But, as to the Etymology of it, I leave that to those who are fond of such unprofitable Disquisitions, though I think this is pretty evident.

When a Design is formed for this Purpose, they go out in Parties from ten to thirty Men, and traverse large Tracts of Mountains, till they arrive at the Place where they intend to commit their Depredations; and that they choose to do as distant as they can from their own Dwellings. The principal Time for this wicked Practice is the Michaelmas Moon, when the Cattle are in Condition fit for Markets, held on the Borders of the Lowlands. They drive the stolen Cows in the Night-Time, and by Day they lie concealed with them in Bye-Places among the Mountains, where hardly any others come; or in Woods, if any such are to be found in their Way.

I must here ask leave to digress a little, and take Notice, that I have several Times used the Word *Cows* for a Drove of Cattle. This is according to the Highland Style; for they say A Drove of Cows, when there are Bulls and Oxen among them, as we say A Flock of Geese, though there be in it many Ganders.

And having just now mentioned the Time of *Lifting*, it revived in my Memory a malicious Saying of the Lowlanders, viz. that the Highland Lairds tell out their Daughters' *Tochers* by the Light of the Michaelmas Moon. But to return:

Sometimes one Band of these Robbers has agreed with another to exchange the stolen Cattle; and, in this Case, they used to commit their Robberies nearer Home; and by appointing a Place of Rendezvous, those that *lifted* in the North-East (for the Purpose) have exchanged with others toward the West, and each have sold them not many Miles from Home, which was commonly at a very great Distance from the Place where they were stolen. Nay, further, as I have been well informed, in making this Contract of Exchange, they have, by Correspondence, long before they went out, described to each other the Colour and Marks of the Cows destined to be stolen and exchanged.

I remember a Story concerning a Highland-Woman, who, begging a Charity of a Lowland Laird's Lady, was asked several Questions; and, among the rest, how many Husbands she had had? To which she answered, three. And being further questioned, if her Husbands had been kind to her, she said the two first were honest Men, and very careful of their Family, for they both *died for the Law*,—that is, were hanged for Theft. " Well, but as to the last?" " Hout!" says she, " a fulthy Peast! he dy'd at Hame, lik an auld Dug, on a *Puckle* o' Strae."

Those that have lost their Cattle sometimes pursue them by the Track, and recover them from the Thieves. Or if in the Pursuit they are *hounded* (as they phrase it) into the Bounds of any other Chief, whose Followers were not concerned in the Robbery, and the Track is there lost, he is obliged by Law to trace them out of his Territory, or make them good to the Owner.

By the Way, the Heath, or Heather, being pressed by the Foot, retains the Impression or at least some remains of it, for a long while, before it rises again effectually; and besides, you know, there are other visible Marks left behind by the Cattle. But even a single Highlander has been found by the Track of his Foot, when he took to Hills out of the common Ways, for his greater Safety in his Flight, as thinking he could not so well be discovered from Hill to Hill, every now and then, as he often might be in the Road (as they call it) between the Mountains.

If the Pursuers overtake the Robbers, and find them inferior in Number, and happen to seize any of them, they are seldom prosecuted, there being but few who are in Circumstances fit to support the Expense of a Prosecution; or,

if they were, they would be liable to have their
Houses burnt, their Cattle hocked, and their
Lives put in Danger, from some of the Clan
to which the Banditti belonged.

But, with the richer Sort, the Chief, or
Chieftain, generally makes a Composition,
when it comes to be well known the Thieves
belonged to his Tribe, which he willingly pays,
to save the Lives of some of his Clan; and
this is repaid him by a Contribution among
the Robbers, who never refuse to do their
utmost to save those of their Fraternity. But
it has been said this Payment has been sometimes made in Cows, stolen from the opposite
Side of the Country, or paid out of the Produce of them when sold at the Market.

It is certain some of the Highlanders think
of this Kind of Depredation as our Deer-
Stealers do of their Park and Forest Enter-
prizes;—that is, to be a small Crime, or none
at all. And, as the latter would think it a
scandalous Reproach to be charged with
robbing a Hen-Roost, so the Highlander

thinks it less shameful to steal a hundred Cows than one single Sheep; for a Sheep-stealer is infamous even among them.

If I am mistaken in that Part of my Account of the *Lifting* of Cattle, which is beyond my own Knowledge, you may lay the Blame to those Gentlemen who gave me the Information.

But there is no more Wonder that Men of Honesty and Probity should disclose, with Abhorrence, the evil Practices of the vile Part of their Countrymen, than that I should confess to them we have, among us, a Number of Villains that cannot plead the least Shadow of an Excuse for their Thievings and Highway-Robberies, unless they could make a Pretence of their Idleness and Luxury.

When I first came into these Parts, a Highland Gentleman, in order to give me a Notion of the Ignorance of some of the ordinary Highlanders, and their Contempt of the Lowland Laws (as they call them), gave me an Account, as we were walking together, of the Behaviour of a common Highlandman at his Trial before the Lords of Justiciary in the Low-Country. By the Way, the Appearance of those Gentlemen upon the Bench is not unlike that of our Judges in England.

I shall repeat the Fellow's Words, as near as I can, by writing in the same broken Accent as my Highland Friend used in mimicking the Criminal.

This Man was accused of stealing, with others, his Accomplices, a good Number of Cattle; and, while his Indictment was in reading, setting forth that he, as a common Thief, had lain in wait, &c., the Highlander lost all Patience, and interrupting, cried out, "Common Tief! common Tief! Steal ane Cow, twa Cow, dat be common Tief: Lift hundred Cow, dat be Shentilman's Trovers." After the Court was again silent, and some little Progress had been made in the Particulars of the Accusation, he again cried out, "Ah, Hone! Dat such fine Shentilmans should sit dere wid der fine Cowns on, to mak a Parshel o' Lees on a peur honesht Mon."

But in Conclusion, when he was told what was to be his Fate he roared out most outrageously, and, fiercely pointing at the Judges, he cried out, " Ah, for a proad-Sword an a Tirk, to rid de Hoose o' tose foul Peastes ! "

Personal Robberies are seldom heard of among them : for my own Part, I have several Times with a single Servant, passed the Mountain-Way from hence to Edinburgh, with four or five hundred Guineas in my Portmanteau, without any Apprehension of Robbers by the Way, or Danger in my Lodgings by Night, though in my Sleep, any one, with Ease, might have thrust a Sword, from the Outside, through the Wall of the Hut and my Body together. I wish we could say as much of our own Country, civilized as it is said to be, though one cannot be safe in going from London to Highgate.

Indeed, in trifling Matters, as a Knife, or some such Thing, which they have Occasion for, and think it will cause no very strict Inquiry, they are some of them, apt to pilfer ;

while a silver Spoon or a Watch might lie in Safety because they have no Means to dispose of either, and to make Use of them would soon discover their Theft. But I cannot approve the Lowland Saying, viz., "Show me a Highlander, and I will show you a Thief."

Yet, after all, I cannot forbear doing Justice upon a certain Laird, whose Lady keeps a *Change* far in the Highlands, west of Town.

This Gentleman, one Day, Opportunity tempting, took a Fancy to the Lock of an Officer's Pistol ; another Time he fell in Love (like many other Men) with a fair but deceitful Outside, in taking the Boss of a Bridle, silvered over, to be all of that valuable Metal. It is true, I never lost any Thing at his Hut ; but the Proverb made me watchful—I need not repeat it.

But let this Account of him be of no Consequence ; for I do assure you, I never knew any one of his Rank do any Thing like it in all the Highlands.

And, for my own Part, I do not remember that ever I lost any Thing among them but a Pair of new Doe-skin Gloves ; and at another Time a Horse-Cloth made of Plaiding, which was taken away while my Horses were swimming across a River ; and that was sent me the next Day to Fort William, to which Place I was going when it was taken from the Rest of my Baggage, as it lay upon the Ground. I say nothing in this Place of another Robbery, because I know the Motive to it was purely Revenge.

I thought I had done with this Part of my Subject ; but there is just now come to my Remembrance a Passage between an ordinary Highlandman and an Officer on Half-pay, who lives in this Town and is himself of Highland Extraction.

He told me, a long while ago, that, on a certain Time, he was going on Foot, and unattended, upon a Visit to a Laird, about seven or eight Miles among the Hills ; and, being clad in a new glossy Summer-Suit (instead of his Highland Dress, which he usually wore upon such Occasions), there overtook him in his Way an ordinary Fellow, who forced himself upon him as a Companion.

When they had gone together about a Mile, his new Fellow-Traveller said to him—"Troth, ye ha getten bra Clais;" of which the Officer took little Notice; but, some Time after, the Fellow began to look sour, and to snort, as they do when they are angry: "Ah, 'tis ponny Geer! what an I sho'd take 'em frae ye noo?" Upon this the Officer drew a Pistol from his Breast, and said, "What do you think of this?"

But at the Sight of the Pistol, the Fellow fell on his Knees, and squalled out, "Ah, hone! ah, hone! she was but shokin."

It is true, this Dialogue passed in Irish, but this is the Language in which I was told the Story.

But I have known several Instances of common Highlanders, who finding themselves like to be worsted, having crouched and howled like a beaten Spaniel, so suddenly has their Insolence been turned into Fawning. But, you know, we have both of us seen, in our own Country, a Change in higher Life not less unmanly.

You may see, by this additional Article, that I can conceal nothing from you, even though it may seem, in some Measure, to call in Question what I had been saying before.

LETTER XXIV.

BESIDES tracking the Cows as mentioned in my last Letter, there was another Means whereby to recover them; which was by sending Persons into the Country suspected, and by them offering a Reward (which they call *Tascal-Money*) to any who should discover the Cattle and those who stole them. This, you may be sure, was done as secretly as possible. The Temptation sometimes, though seldom, proved too strong to be resisted; and the Cattle being thereby discovered, a Restitution, or other Satisfaction, was obtained. But, to put a Stop to a Practice so detrimental to their Interest and dangerous to their Persons, the thievish Part of the Camerons, and others afterwards, by their Example, bound themselves by Oath never to receive any such Reward, or inform one against another.

This Oath they take upon a drawn Dirk, which they kiss in a solemn Manner consenting, if ever they prove perjured, to be stabbed with the same Weapon, or any other of the like Sort.

Hence they think no Wickedness so great as the Breach of this Oath, since they hope for Impunity in committing almost every other Crime, and are so certainly and severely punished for this Transgression.

An Instance of their Severity in this Point happened in December 1723, when one of the said Camerons, suspected of having taken Tascal-Money, was, in the Dead of the Night, called out of his Hut from his Wife and Children, and, under Pretence of some new Enterprize, allured to some Distance, out of hearing, and there murdered: and another, for the same Crime, as they call it, was either thrown down some Precipice, or otherwise made away with, for he was never heard of afterwards.

Having mentioned above the Manner of

taking their Oath, relating to Tascal-Money, I shall here give you a Specimen of a Highland Oath upon other Occasions; in taking whereof they do not kiss the Book, as in England, but hold up their right Hand, saying thus, or to this Purpose:

"By God himself, and as I shall answer to God at the great Day, I shall speak the Truth: if I do not, may I never thrive while I live; may I go to Hell and be damned when I die. May my Land bear neither Grass nor Corn: may my Wife and Bairns never prosper; may my Cows, Calves, Sheep, and Lambs, all perish," &c.

I say to this Purpose, for I never heard they had any established Form of an Oath among them. Besides, you perceive it must necessarily be varied according to the Circumstances of the Person who swears, at the Discretion of him who administers the Oath.

When the Chief was an Encourager of this Kind of Theft, which I have the Charity to believe was uncommon, and the Robbers succeeded in their Attempt, he received two-Thirds of the Spoil, or the Produce of it; and the remaining third Part was divided among the Thieves.

The Clans that had among them the most of Villains addicted to these Robberies are said, by the People bordering on the Highlands, to be the Camerons, Mackenzies, the Broadalbinmen, the M'Gregors, and the M'Donalds of Keppock and Glenco. The Chieftain of these last is said, by his near Neighbours, to have little besides those Depredations for his Support; and the Chief of the first, whose Clan has been particularly stigmatized for those Violences, has, as I am very well informed, strictly forbidden any such vile Practices, which has not at all recommended him to some of his Followers.

Besides these ill-minded People among the Clans, there are some Stragglers in the Hills, who, like our Gypsies, have no certain Habitation, only they do not stroll about in Numbers

like them. These go singly, and, though perfectly unknown, do not beg at the Door, but,
without Invitation or formal Leave, go into a
Hut, and sit themselves down by the Fire, ex-
pecting to be supplied with Oatmeal for their
present Food. When Bed-time comes, they
wrap themselves up in their Plaids, or beg the
Use of a Blanket, if any to be spared, for their
Covering, and then lay themselves down upon
the Ground in some Corner of the Hut. Thus
the Man and his Wife are often deprived of
the Freedom of their own Habitation, and
cannot be alone together. But the Inhabitants
are in little Danger of being pilfered by these
Guests—nor, indeed, do they seem to be
apprehensive of it; for not only there is
generally little to be stolen, but, if they took
some small Matter, it would be of no Use to
the Thief for want of a Receiver; and, besides, they would be pursued and easily taken.
The People say themselves, if it were not for
this Connivance of theirs, by a Kind of
customary Hospitality, these Wanderers would

soon be starved, having no Money wherewith to purchase Sustenance.

But I have heard great Complaint of this Custom from a Highland Farmer of more than ordinary Substance, at whose Dwelling I happened to see an Instance of this Intrusion, it being very near to the Place where I resided for a Time; and he told me he should think himself happy if he was taxed at any Kind of reasonable Rate, to be freed from this great Inconvenience.

Above I have given you a Sketch of the Highland Oath, and here I shall observe to you how slightly a certain Highlander thought of the Lowland Form.

This Man was brought as a Witness against another in a supposed criminal Case : the Magistrate tendered him the Low-Country Oath, and, seeing the Fellow addressing himself confidently to take it, though he greatly suspected, by several Circumstances, the Man was suborned, changed his Method, and offered him the Highland Oath—" No," says the Highlander, "I cannot do that, for I will not forswear myself to please anybody!"

This single Example might be sufficient to show how necessary it is to swear the common People in the Method of their own Country; yet, by Way of Chat, I shall give you another, though it be less different in the Fact than in the Expression.

At Carlisle Assizes, a Highlandman, who had meditated the Ruin of another, prosecuted him for Horse-stealing, and swore positively to the Fact.

This being done, the supposed Criminal desired his Prosecutor might be sworn in the Highland Manner; and, the Oath being tendered him accordingly, he refused it, saying, "Thar is a hantle o' Difference betwixt blawing on a Buke and dam'ing one's Saul."

But I have heard of several other Examples of the same Kind, notwithstanding the Oath taken in the Low-Country has the same Introduction, viz. "By God, and as I shall answer,

&c." but then the Land, Wife, Children and Cattle, are not concerned; for there is no Imprecation in it either upon them or him that takes the Oath.

As most People, when they begin to grow in Years, are unwilling to think themselves incapable of their former Pleasures, so some of the Highland Gentlemen seem to imagine they still retain that exorbitant Power which they formerly exercised over the Lives of their Vassals and Followers, even without legal Trial and Examination. Of this Power I have heard several of them vaunt; but it might be Ostentation:—however, I shall mention one in particular.

I happened to be at the House of a certain Chief, when the Chieftain of a Tribe belonging to another Clan came to make a Visit; after talking of indifferent Matters, I told him I thought some of his People had not behaved toward me, in a particular Affair, with that Civility I might have expected from the Clan. He started; and immediately, with an Air of

Fierceness, clapped his Hand on his broad-
Sword, and told me, if I required it, he would
send me two or three of their Heads.

But I, really thinking he had been in Jest,
and had acted well (as Jesting is not their
Talent), laughed out, by Way of Approbation
of his Capacity for a Joke; upon which he
assumed if possible, a yet more serious Look,
and told me peremptorily *he was a Man of his
Word;* and the Chief who sat by made no
Manner of Objection to what he said.

The heritable Power of *Pit and Gallows,* as
they call it, which still is exercised by some
within their proper Districts, is, I think, too
much for any particular Subject to be entrusted
withal. But it is said that any Partiality or
Revenge of the Chief, in his own Cause, is
obviated by the Law, which does not allow
himself to sit judicially, but obliges him to
appoint a Substitute as Judge in his Courts,
who is called the *Baily of Regality.*

I fear this is but a Shadow of Safety to the
accused, if it may not appear to increase the

Danger of Injustice and Oppression; for to the Orders and Instructions of the Chief may be added the private Resentment of the Baily, which may make up a double Weight against the supposed Criminal.

I have not, I must own, been accustomed to hear Trials in these Courts, but have been often told, that one of these Bailies, in particular, seldom examines any but with raging Words and Rancour; and, if the Answers made are not to his Mind, he contradicts them by Blows; and, one Time, even to the knocking down of the poor Wretch who was examined. Nay, further, I have heard say of him, by a very credible Person, that a Highlander of a neighbouring Clan, with whom his own had been long at Variance, being to be brought before him, he declared upon the Accusation, before he had seen the Party accused, *that the very Name should hang him.*

I have not mentioned this violent and arbitrary Proceeding as though I knew or thought it usual in those Courts, but to show how little

Mankind in general are to be trusted with a lawless Power, to which there is no other Check or Control but good Sense and Humanity, which are not common enough to restrain every one who is invested with such Power, as appears by this Example.

The Baily of Regality, in many Cases, takes upon him the same State as the Chief himself would do;—as for one single Instance.

When he travels, in Time of Snow, the Inhabitants of one Village must walk before him to make a Path to the next; and so on to the End of his Progress: and, in a dark Night, they light him from one inhabited Place to another, which are mostly far distant, by carrying blazing Sticks of Fir.

Formerly the Power assumed by the Chief in remote Parts was perfectly despotic, of which I shall only mention what was told me by a near Relation of a certain attainted Lord, whose Estate (that was) lies in the Northern Highlands; but hold—this Moment, upon Recollection, I have resolved to add to it an

Example of the arbitrary Proceeding of one much less powerful than the Chief, who nevertheless thought he might dispose of the Lives of Foreigners at his Pleasure. As to the first, —the Father of the late Earl above-mentioned having a great Desire to get a Fellow apprehended, who was said to have been guilty of many atrocious Crimes, set a Price upon his Head of one hundred and twenty Crowns (a Species of Scots Coin in those Days),—I suppose about Five-pence or Six-pence, and, of his own Authority, gave Orders for taking him alive or dead; that the Pursuers, thinking it dangerous to themselves to attempt the securing him alive, shot him, and brought his Head and one of his Hands to the Chief, and immediately received the promised Reward. The other is as follows:—

I remember to have heard, a good while ago, that in the time when Prince George of Denmark was Lord-High-Admiral of England, some Scots Gentlemen represented to him, that Scotland could furnish the Navy with as good

Timber for Masts and other Uses as either Sweden or Norway could do, and at a much more reasonable Rate.

This succeeded so far that two Surveyors were sent to examine into the Allegations of their Memorial.

Those Gentlemen came first to Edinburgh, where they staid some time to concert the rest of their Journey, and to learn from the Inhabitants their Opinion concerning the Execution of their Commission, among whom there was one Gentleman that had some Acquaintance with a certain Chieftain in a very remote Part of the Highlands, and he gave them a Letter to him.

They arrived at the Laird's House, declared the Cause of their coming, and produced their Credentials, which were a Warrant and Instructions from the Prince; but the Chieftain, after perusing them, told them he knew nothing of any such Person. They then told him he was Husband to Queen Anne; and he answered, he knew nothing of either of them; " But," says he, " there came hither, some

Time ago, such as you from Ireland, as Spies upon the Country, and we hear they have made their Jests upon us among the Irish.

"Now," says he, "you shall have one Hour; and if in that time you can give me no better Account of yourselves than you have hitherto done, I'll hang you both upon that Tree." Upon which his Attendants showed great Readiness to execute his Orders: and, in this Perplexity, he abruptly left them, without seeing the Edinburgh Letter; for of that they made but little Account, since the Authority of the Prince, and even the Queen, were to him of no Consequence: but afterwards, as they were walking backwards and forwards in the Garden counting the Minutes, one of them resolved to try what the Letter might do: this was agreed to by the other, as the last Resort; but, in the Hurry and Confusion they were in, it was not for some Time to be found, being worked into a Corner of the Bearer's usual Pocket, and so he passed to another, &c.,

Now the Hour is expired, and the haughty Chieftain enters the Garden; and one of them gave him the Letter: this he read, and then turning to them, said, " Why did not you produce this at first? If you had not had it, I should most certainly have hanged you both immediately."

The Scene being thus changed, he took them into his House, gave them Refreshment, and told them they might take a Survey of his Woods the next Morning, or when they thought fit.

There is one Chief who sticks at nothing to gratify his Avarice or Revenge.

This Oppressor, upon the least Offence or Provocation, makes no Conscience of hiring Villains out of another Clan, as he has done several Times, to execute his diabolical Purposes by hocking of Cattle, burning of Houses, and even to commit Murder itself. Out of many Enormities, I shall only mention two.

The first was,—that being Offended, though very unreasonably, with a Gentleman, even of his own Name and Clan, he, by horrid Commerce with one who governed another Tribe in the Absence of his Chief, agreed with him for a Parcel of Assassins to murder his Vassal, and bring him, his Head, I suppose, as a Voucher. The Person devoted to Death, happened to be absent the Night the Murderers came to his House, and therefore the Villains resolved not to go away empty-handed, but to take his Daughter's Head in lieu of his own; which the poor Creature perceiving, was frighted to such a Degree, that she has not recovered her Understanding to this Day.

The Servant-Maid they abused with a Dirk in a butcherly Manner, too shameful to be described: to be short, the Neighbours, though at some Distance, hearing the Cries and Shrieks of the Females, took the Alarm, and the inhuman Monsters made their Escape.

The other Violence related to a Gentleman who lives near this Town, and was appointed Umpire in a litigated Affair by the Chief and the other Party; and, because this Laird thought he could not, with any Colour of Justice, decide in favour of the Chief, his Cattle, that were not far from his House, were some hocked and the rest of them killed; but the Owner of them, as the other, was absent that Night, in all Probability suspecting (or having some private Intelligence of) his Danger; and, when this horrid Butchery was finished, the Ruffians went to his House, and wantonly diverted themselves in telling the Servants they had done their Master a good Piece of Service, for they had saved him the Expense of a Butcher to kill his Cattle: and I have been told, that the next Morning there were seen a Number of Calves sucking at the Dugs of the dead Cows. But two of them were afterwards apprehended and executed.

These Men (as is said of Coleman) were allured to Secrecy while under Condemnation, though sometimes inclined to confess their Employer; and thus they continued to depend upon Promises till the Knot was tied; and then it was too late: but all manner of Circumstances were too flagrant to admit a Doubt concerning the first Instigator of their Wickedness; yet few of the neighbouring Inhabitants dare to trust one another with their Sentiments of it.

But here comes the finishing Stroke to the first of these execrable Pieces of Workmanship.

Not long after the vile Attempt, he who had furnished the Murderers made a Demand on the Chief of a certain Quantity of Oatmeal, which was to be the Price of the Assassination; but, in Answer, he was told, if he would send Money, it might be had of a Merchant with whom he (the Chief) had frequent Dealings; and as for himself, he had but just enough for his own Family till the next Crop.

This shuffling Refusal occasioned the Threats of a Law-suit; but the Demander was told, the Business had not been effectually performed; and besides, as he knew the Consideration, he might commence his Process, and declare it in a Court as soon as ever he thought fit.

This last Circumstance I did not, or perhaps could not, know till lately, when I was in that Part of the Highlands from whence the Villains were hired.

I must again apologize, and say, I make no Doubt you will take this Account (as it is intended) to be a Piece of historical Justice done upon one who is lawless, and deserves much more, and not as a Sample of a Highland Chief, or the least Imputation on any other of those Gentlemen.

Yet Truth obliges me to confess, that in some Parts there remains among the Natives a kind of Spanish or Italian Inclination to revenge themselves, as it were, by Proxy, of those who they think have injured them, or interfered with their Interest. This I could not but infer, soon after my Coming to the western Parts of the Highlands, from the saying of a Youth, Son of a Laird in the Neighbourhood.

He was telling me his Father's Estate had been much embarrassed, but, by a lucky Hit,

II.   R

a Part of it was redeemed. I was desirous to know by what Means, and he proceeded to tell me there were two Wadsets upon it, and both of the Mortgagees had been in Possession, each claiming a Right to about half; but one of them being a Native, and the other a Stranger,—that is, not of the Clan, the former had taken the latter aside, and told him if he did not immediately quit the Country, he would hang him upon the next Tree. "What !" says a Highlander who was born in the East, and went with me into those Parts, "that would be the way to be hanged himself." "Out !" says the Youth, "you talk as if you did not know your own Country :— that would have been done, and nobody knew who did it." This he spoke with an Air as if he had been talking of ordinary Business, and was angry with the other for being ignorant of it, who afterwards owned that my Presence was the Cause of his Objection.

Besides what I have recounted in this Letter, which might serve as an Indication that some, at least, of the ordinary Highlanders are not averse to the Price of Blood, I shall here take notice of a Proposal of that Kind which was made to myself.

Having given the Preference to a certain Clan in a profitable Business, it brought upon me the Resentment of the Chieftain of a small neighbouring Tribe, Part of a Clan at Enmity with the former.

This Gentleman thought his People had as much Right to my Favour in that Particular as the other: the first Instance of his Revenge was a Robbery committed by one of his Tribe, whom I ordered to be *hounded out*, and he was taken. This Fellow I resolved to prosecute to the utmost, which brought the Chieftain to solicit me in his Behalf.

He told me, for Introduction, that it was not usual in the Hills for Gentlemen to carry such Matters to Extremity, but rather to accept of a Composition: and, finding their Custom of compounding had no Weight with me, he offered a Restitution; but I was firmly resolved, *in terrorem*, to punish the Thief. Seeing this Proposal was likewise ineffectual, he told me the Man's Wife was one of the prettiest young Women in the Highlands, and if I would pardon the Husband I should *have her*.

I told him that was an agreeable Bribe, yet it could not prevail over the Reasons I had to refer the Affair to Justice.

Some time after, a Highlander came privately to me, and, by my own Interpreter, told me he heard I had a Quarrel with the Laird of——— and if that was true, he thought *he had lived long enough* ; but not readily apprehending his Intention, I asked the Meaning of that dubious Expression, and was answered, he would kill him for me if I would encourage it. The Proposal really surprised me ; but soon recovering myself, I ordered him to be told, that I believed he was a trusty honest Man, and if I had Occasion for such Service, I should employ him before any other, but it was the Custom in my Country, when two Gentlemen had a

Quarrel, to go into the Field and Decide it between themselves.

At the Interpretation of this last Part of my Speech, he shook his Head and said, " What a Foolish Custom is that!"

Perhaps this Narration, as well as some others that have preceded, may be thought to consist of too many Circumstances, and, consequently to be of an unnecessary Length ; but I hope there are none that do not, by that Means, convey the Knowledge of some Custom or Inclination of the People, which otherwise might have been omitted ; besides, I am myself, as you know very well, an Enemy to long Stories.

Some of the Highland Gentlemen are immoderate Drinkers of Usky,—even three or four Quarts at a Sitting ; and, in general, the People that can pay the Purchase, drink it without Moderation.

Not long ago, four English Officers took a Fancy to try their Strength in this Bow of Ulysses, against the like Number of the

Country Champions, but the Enemy came off victorious ; and one of the Officers was thrown into a Fit of the Gout, without Hopes; another had a most dangerous Fever, a third lost his Skin and Hair by the Surfeit ; and the last confessed to me, that when Drunkenness and Debate ran high he took several Opportunities to sham it.

They say, for Excuse, the Country requires a great deal ; but I think they mistake a Habit and Custom for Necessity. They like-wise pretend it does not intoxicate in the Hills as it would do in the Low-Country ; but this I also doubt, by their own Practice ; for those among them who have any Consideration, will hardly care so much as to refresh themselves with it, when they pass near the Tops of the Mountains : for, in that Circumstance, they say it renders them careless, listless of the Fatigue, and inclined to sit down, which might invite to Sleep, and then they would be in Danger to perish with the Cold. I have been tempted to think this Spirit has in it, by Infusion, the Seeds of Anger, Revenge, and Murder (this I confess is a little too poetical) ; but those who drink of it to any Degree of Excess behave, for the most Part, like true Barbarians, I think much beyond the Effect of other Liquors.   The Collector of the Customs at Stornway, in the Isle of Lewis, told me, that about one hundred and twenty Families drink yearly four thousand English Gallons of this Spirit and Brandy together, although many of them are so poor they cannot afford to pay for much of either, which, you know, must increase the Quantity drank by the rest ; and that they frequently give to Children of six or seven Years old as much at a Time as an ordinary Wine Glass would hold.

When they choose to qualify it for Punch, they sometimes mix it with Water and Honey, or with Milk and Honey ; at other times the Mixture is only the *Aqua Vitæ*, Sugar, and Butter ; this they burn till the Butter and Sugar are dissolved.

The Air of the Highlands is pure, and consequently Healthy; insomuch that I have known such Cures done by it as might be thought next to Miracles;—I mean in Distempers of the Lungs, as Coughs, Consumptions, &c.

And as I have mentioned the Honey above, I shall here give that its due Commendation; I think, then, it is in every respect as good as that of Minorca, so much esteemed, and both, I suppose, are in a great Measure produced from the bloom of the Heath; for which Reason, too, our Hampshire Honey is more valued than any from other Parts near London, because that County is mostly covered with Heath.

As the Lowlanders call their Part of the Country the Land of Cakes, so the Natives of the Hills say they inhabit a Land of Milk and Honey.

P. S. In the Low Country the Cakes are called *Cookies;* and the several Species of them, of which there are many, though not much differing in Quality one from another, are

dignified and distinguished by the Names of
the reigning Toasts, or the good Housewife
who was the Inventor,—as for example, Lady
Cullen's Cookies, &c.

LETTER XXV.

IN a former Letter, I ventured to give it you as my Opinion, that Mankind in different Countries are naturally the same. I shall now send you a short Sketch of what I have observed in the Conversation of an English Fox-hunter and that of a Highland Laird, supposing neither of them to have had a liberal and polite Education, or to have been far out of their own Countries.

The first of these Characters is, I own, too trite to be given you—but this by Way of Comparison:

The Squire is proud of his Estate and Affluence of Fortune, loud and positive over his October, impatient of Contradiction, or rather will give no Opportunity for it, but Whoops and Halloos at every Interval of his own Talk, as if the Company were to supply the Absence of his Hounds.

The particular Characters of the Pack, the various Occurrences in a Chase, where Jowler is the eternal Hero, make the constant Topic of his Discourse, though, perhaps, none others are interested in it; and his Favourites, the Trencher-Hounds, if they please, may lie undisturbed upon Chairs and Counterpanes of Silk; and, upon the least Cry, though not hurt, his Pity is excited more for them than if one of his Children had broken a Limb; and to that Pity his Anger succeeds, to the Terror of the whole Family.

The Laird is national, vain of the Number of his Followers and his absolute Command over them. In case of Contradiction, he is loud and imperious, and even dangerous, being always attended by those who are bound to support his arbitrary Sentiments.

The great Antiquity of his Family, and the heroic Actions of his Ancestors, in their Conquest of Enemy Clans, is the inexhaustible

Theme of his Conversation; and, being accustomed to Dominion, he imagines himself, in his Usky, to be a sovereign Prince; and, as I said before, fancies he may dispose of Heads at his Pleasure.

Thus one of them places his Vanity in his Fortune, and his Pleasure in his Hounds; the other's Pride is in his Lineage, and his Delight is command—both arbitrary in their Way; and this the Excess of Liquor discovers in both; so that what little Difference there is between them seems to arise from the Accident of their Birth; and, if the Exchange of Countries had been made in their Infancy, I make no Doubt but each might have had the other's Place, as they stand separately described in this Letter.

On the contrary, in like Manner, as we have many Country Gentlemen, merely such, of great Humanity and agreeable (if not general) Conversation; so in the Highlands I have met with some Lairds, who surprised me with their good Sense and polite Behaviour, being so far removed from the more civilized Part of the World, and considering the Wildness of the Country, which one would think was sufficient of itself to give a savage Turn to a Mind the most humane.

The Isles to the North-West and to the North of the main Land (if I may so speak of this our Island) may not improperly be called Highlands; for they are mountainous, and the Natives speak the Language, follow the Customs, and wear the Habit of the High-landers.

In some of the Western Islands (as well as in Part of the Highlands), the People never rub out a greater Quantity of Oats than what is just necessary for Seed against the following Year; the rest they reserve in the Sheaves, for their Food; and, as they have Occasion, set Fire to some of them, not only to dry the Oats, which, for the most Part, are wet, but to burn off the Husk. Then, by winnowing, they separate, as well as they can, the sooty Part from the Grain; but as this cannot be done effectually, the *Bannack*, or Cake they make of it, is very black. Thus they deprive themselves of the Use of Straw, leaving none to thatch their Huts, make their Beds, or feed their Cattle in the Winter Season.

They seldom burn and grind a greater Quantity of these Oats than serves for a Day, except on a Saturday; when some will prepare a double Portion, that they may have nothing to do on the Sunday following. This Oatmeal is called *Graydon Meal.*

For Grinding the Oats, they have a Machine they call a *Quarn.* This is composed of two Stones; the undermost is about a Foot and a Half or two Feet Diameter. It is round, and five or six inches deep in the Hollow, like an earthen Pan. Within this they place another Stone, pretty equal at the Edge to that Hollow. This last is flat, like a wooden Pot-lid, about three or four Inches thick, and in the Centre of it is a pretty large round Hole, which goes quite through, whereby to convey the Oats between the Stones: there are also two or three Holes in different Places, near the extreme Part of the Surface, that go about Half-way through the Thickness, which is just Deep enough to keep a Stick in its Place, by which, with the Hand, they turn it round and round, till they have finished the Operation. But in a wild Part of Argyleshire, there was no Bread of any Kind till the Discovery of some Lead-Mines, which brought Strangers among the Inhabitants; who before fed upon the Milk of their Cows, Goats, and Sheep.

In Summer they used to shake their Milk in a Vessel, till it was very frothy, which puffed them up, and satisfied them for the present; and their Cheese served them instead of Bread. The Reason why they had no Bread was, that there is hardly any arable Land for a great Space, all round about that Part of the Country.

I have been assured, that in some of the Islands the meaner Sort of People still retain the Custom of boiling their Beef in the Hide; or otherwise (being destitute of Vessels of

Metal or Earth) they put Water into a Block
of Wood, made hollow by the help of the
Dirk and burning; and then with pretty large
Stones heated red-hot, and successively
quenched in that Vessel, they keep the
Water boiling till they have dressed their
Food. It is said, likewise, that they roast a
Fowl in the Embers, with the Guts and
Feathers; and when they think it done
enough, they strip off the Skin, and then
think it fit for the Table.

A Gentleman of my Acquaintance told me,
that, in coming from Ireland to the Western
Highlands, he was reduced, by an Ague, to
the Necessity of landing upon the Island
Macormach; and, arriving at the public
Change, he observed three Quarters of a Cow
to lie in a shallow Part of the Salt Water,
and the other Quarter hanging up against the
End of the Hut; that, asking the Reason of
it, he was told they had no Salt; and it was
their Way of preserving their Beef.

Some Time after, the Woman of the Hut

(or the *guid Wife*) took a Side of a Calf that
had been taken out of the Cow, and, holding
it by the Legs, waved it backward and forward over the Fire till Part of it was roasted,
as she thought, and then tore off one of the
Limbs, and offered it to him to eat.   A
tempting Dish! especially for a sick Stomach!

It is often said, that some of the Lairds of
those Islands take upon them the State of Mo-
narchs; and thence their Vassals have a great
Opinion of their Power.

Among other Stories told of them, there is
one pretty well known in the North of Scotland, but whether true, or feigned as a
Ridicule upon them, I do not know.   For
notwithstanding the Lowland Scots complain
of the English for ridiculing other Nations,
yet they themselves have a great Number of
standing Jokes upon the Highlanders.

They say a Spanish Ship being stranded
upon the Coast of Barra (a very small Island
to the South of Lewes), the Chief (M'Neil)
called a Council of his Followers, which, I

II.   S

think, they say were about fifty in Number, in order to determine what was to be done with her; that, in the course of the Consultation, one of the Members proposed, "If she was laden with Wine and Brandy, she should be confiscated as an illicit Trader upon the Coast, but if she was freighted with other Merchandise, they should plunder her as a Wreck."

Upon this, one of the Council, more cautious than the rest, objected that the King of Spain might resent such Treatment of his Subjects; but the other replied, "We have nothing to do with that; M'Neil and the King of Spain will adjust that Matter between themselves."

As this is a cold Country, the People endeavour to vail themselves of the Condition of those who live in a more northern Climate.

They tell you that some of the Lairds in the Islands of Shetland, which are far North of the Orkneys, hire a Domestic by the half-Year, or by the Quarter, just as they can agree, whose Business it is to put an Instru-

ment in Order when the Laird has an Inclination to play upon it, but if he attempts to play
a Tune himself, he is sure to be discarded.

Of this they give you an Instance in a certain Laird, who, observing his Servant went
farther toward an *Air* than he ought to have
done by Agreement (perhaps vainly imagining
he could play better than his Master), he had
Warning to provide himself with another
Service against the next Martinmas, which
was then about two Months to come. And,
although the Man was not suspended, in the
mean Time, from the Exercise of his Function
(because he was to be paid for the whole
Time), yet in all that Interval no Manner of
Intercession could prevail with the Laird to
continue him in his Service beyond that
Quarter :—no, notwithstanding his own Lady
strongly solicited him in Behalf of the poor
unhappy Offender; nor could she obtain so
much as a Certificate in his Favour.

Here you will say, all this must be a
Riddle ; and, indeed, so it is. But your

Friend Sir Alexander, or any other of your Scots Acquaintance, can explain it to you much better over a Bottle, or walking in St. James's Park, than I can do upon Paper. They can likewise give you the Title of the *Hireling*, which I have forgot; and, when all that is done, I dare venture to say, you will conclude there is no Occasion for such an Officer in any English Family. And, for my own Part, I really think there is as little Need of him anywhere on this Side the Tweed within the Compass of the Ocean.

We had the other Day, in our Coffee-Room, an Auction of Books, if such Trash, and so small a Number of them, may go by that Name.

One of them I purchased, which I do not re-member to have ever heard of before, although it was published so long ago as the Year 1703.

It is a Description of the Western Islands of Scotland, and came extremely *à propos*, to pre-vent my saying any Thing further concerning them.

I have nothing to object against the
Author's (Mr Martin's) Account of those
Isles, with Respect to their Situation, Mountains, Lakes, Rivers, Caves, &c. For I confess I never was in any one of them, though I
have seen several of them from the main Land.
But I must observe, that to furnish out his
Book with much of the *wonderful* (a Quality
necessary to all Books of Travels, and it would
be happy if History were less tainted with it),
he recounts a great Variety of strange Customs
used by the Natives (if ever in Use) in Days of
yore, with many other Wonders ; among all
which the *second Sight* is the superlative.

This, he says, is a Faculty, Gift, or Misfortune (for he mentions it under those three
Predicaments), whereby all those who are
possessed of it, or by it, see the perfect Images
of absent Objects, either human, brute, vegetable, artificial, &c. And if there be fifty
other Persons in the same Place, those Sights
are invisible to them all : nor even are they
seen by any one who has himself, at other

Times, the *second Sight*, unless the Person who has the Faculty, at that Instant, should touch him with Design to communicate it to him.

It is not peculiar to adult Persons, but is sometimes given to young Children. Women have this supernatural Sight, and even Horses and Cows. It is Pity he does not tell us how those two Kinds of Cattle distinguish between natural and preternatural Appearances, so as to be fearless of the one and affrighted at the other, though seemingly the same; and how all this came to be known.

Upon this Subject he employs six and thirty Pages, *i.e.*, a small Part of them in re-counting what Kind of Appearances forebode Death, which of them are Presages of Marriage, &c., as though it were a settled System.

The remaining Leaves are taken up in Examples of such prophetic Apparitions and the Certainty of their Events.

But I shall trouble you no further with so contemptible a Subject, or myself with pointing out the Marks of Imposture, except to add one Remark, which is, that this ridiculous Notion has almost excluded another, altogether as weak and frivolous ; for he mentions only two or three slight Suspicions of *Witchcraft*, but not one Fact of that Nature throughout his whole Book. Yet both this and second Sight are sprung from one and the same Stock, which I suppose to be very ancient, as they are Children of *Credulity*, who was begotten by *Superstition*, who was the Offspring of *Craft* ; —but you must make out the next Ancestor yourself, for his Name is torn off from the Pedigree, but I believe he was the Founder of the Family.

In looking upwards to what I have been writing, I have paused awhile to consider what it was that could induce me to detain you so long about this trifling Matter ; and at last I have resolved it into a Love of Truth, which is naturally communicative, and makes it painful to conceal the Impositions of Falsehood. But these Islands are so remote and unfrequented, they are a very proper Subject for Invention ; and few, I think, would have the Curiosity to visit them, in order to disprove any Account of them, however romantic.

I can make no other Apology for the Length of this Detail, because I might have gone a much shorter Way, by only mentioning the Book, and hinting its Character; and so leaving it to your Choice, whether to take Notice of it or reject it.

This Letter will bring you the Conclusion of our *Correspondence,* so far as it relates to this Part of our Island; yet if any Thing should happen hereafter that may be thought qualified to go upon its Travels five hundred Miles Southward, it will be a Pleasure to me to give it the necessary Despatch.

I have called it *Correspondence,* from the Remarks I have received from you upon such Passages in my Letters as gave you the Occasion : and I wish my Subject would have enabled me to give you Opportunities to increase their Number.

Writers, you know, for the most Part, have not been contented with any Thing less than the Characters and Actions of those whom Birth or Fortune had set up to public View, or the Policy or Weakness of public Councils; the Order and Event of Battles, Sieges, and such like, in great Measure dressed up in Habits cut out by themselves; but the Genius of a People has been thought beneath their Notice.

This, forsooth, is called supporting the Dignity of History. Now, in this Case, who shall condescend to give a Detail of Circumstances generally esteemed to be low, and therefore of little Consequence, and at the same Time escape the Character of a Trifler?

But I am unwarily fallen into an Apology to you, and not as if I was writing *en Confidence* to a Friend, but openly to the whole Kingdom.

For my own Part (who have already lived too long to be dazzled with glittering Appearances), I should be as well pleased to see a

Shepherd of Arcadia, free from poetial Fiction, in his rustic Behaviour and little Economy, or a Burgher of ancient Rome in his Shop, as to know the Character of a Consul; for, in either Case, it is the Comparison of past Ages, and foreign Countries opposed to our own, that excites my Curiosity and gives me Satisfaction.

As we are now about to settle our Accounts to this Time, I shall acknowledge (as every honest Man would do) the Value of an Article which, it is likely, you make little Account of, as the Indians are said to have done of their Gold when they gave it away for Baubles,— and that is, the agreeable Amusement you have furnished me with, from Time to Time, concerning such Passages as could not, for good Reasons, be admitted to the public Papers. This to one almost excluded the World may, in some Measure, be said to restore him to his native Home.

Upon the whole, when all the Articles in your Favour are brought to Account, I think the Balance will be on your Side; and yet I make no Doubt you would cheerfully go on to increase the Debt, though I should become a Bankrupt, and there did not remain to you the least Expectation of Payment from, &c.

LETTER XXVI.

Concerning the New Roads, &c., 173—

IT is now about eight Years since I sent you the Conclusion of my rambling Account of the Highlands; and, perhaps, you would not have complained if, in this long Interval, you had been perfectly free of so barren a Subject.

Monsieur Fontenelle, I remember, in one of his pastoral Dialogues, makes a Shepherd object to another—*Quoi! toujours de l' Amour?* And I think you may as well ask—What! always Highlands? But in my Situation, without them, I should be in the sorrowful Condition of an old Woman in her Country Cottage, by a Winter Fire, and nobody would hearken to her Tales of Witches and Spirits;—that is, to have little or nothing to say. But now I am a perfect Volunteer, and cannot plead my former Excuses, and really am without any Apprehensions of being thought officious in giving you some Account of the Roads, which, within these few Weeks, have been completely finished.

These new Roads were begun in the Year 1726, and have continued about eleven Years in the Prosecution; yet, long as it may be thought, if you were to pass over the whole Work (for the Borders of it would show you what it was), I make no Doubt but that Number of Years would diminish in your Imagination to a much shorter Tract of Time, by Comparison with the Difficulties that attended the Execution.

But, before I proceed to any particular Descriptions of them, I shall inform you how they lie, to the End that you may trace them out upon a Map of Scotland; and first I shall take them as they are made, to enter the Mountains, viz.

One of them begins from Crief, which is

about fourteen Miles from Stirling : here the
Romans left off their Works, of which some
Parts are visible to this Day, particularly the
Camp at Ardoch, where the Vestiges of the
Fortifications are on a Moor so barren, that its
whole Form has been safe from Culture, or
other Alteration besides Weather and Time.

The other Road enters the Hills at Dimheld,
in Athol, which is about ten Miles from Perth.

The first of them, according to my Account,
though the last in Execution, proceeds through
Glenalmond (which, for its Narrowness, and
the Height of the Mountains, I remember to
have mentioned formerly), and thence it goes
to Aberfaldy; there it crosses the River Tay
by a Bridge of Free-Stone, consisting of five
spacious Arches (by the Way, this military
Bridge is the only Passage over that wild and
dangerous River), and from thence the Road
goes on to Dalnachardoch.

The other Road from Dunkeld proceeds by
the Blair of Athol to the said Dalnachardoch.

Here the two Roads join in one, and, as a

single Road, it leads on to Dalwhinny, where it branches out again into two; of which one proceeds towards the North-West, through Garva-Moor, and over the Coriarach Mountain to Fort Augustus, at Killichumen, and the other Branch goes due North to the Barrack of Ruthven, in Badenoch, and thence, by Delmagary, to Inverness. From thence it proceeds something to the Southward of the West, across the Island, to the aforesaid Fort-Augustus, and so on to Fort-William, in Lochaber.

The Length of all these Roads put together is about two hundred and fifty Miles.

I have so lately mentioned Glenalmond, in the Road from Crief, Northward, that I cannot forbear a Digression, though at my first setting out, in relation to a Piece of Antiquity which happened to be discovered in that Vale not many Hours before I passed through it in one of my Journeys southward.

A small Part of the Way through this Glen having been marked out by two Rows of

Camp-Colours, placed at a good Distance one from another, whereby to describe the Line of the intended Breadth and Regularity of the Road by the Eye, there happened to lie directly in the way an exceedingly large Stone, and, as it had been made a Rule from the Beginning, to carry on the Roads in straight Lines, as far as the Way would permit, not only to give them a better Air, but to shorten the Passenger's Journey, it was resolved the Stone should be removed, if possible, though otherwise the Work might have been carried along on either Side of it.

The Soldiers, by vast Labour, with their Levers and Jacks, or Hand-screws, tumbled it over and over till they got it quite out of the Way, although it was of such an enormous Size that it might be Matter of great Wonder how it could ever be removed by human Strength and Art, especially to such who had never seen an Operation of that Kind : and, upon their digging a little Way into that Part of the Ground where the Centre of the Base had stood, there was found a small Cavity, about two Feet square, which was guarded from the outward Earth at the Bottom, Top, and Sides, by square flat Stones.

This Hollow contained some Ashes, Scraps of Bones, and half-burnt Ends of Stalks of Heath ; which last we concluded to be a small Remnant of a Funeral Pile. Upon the whole, I think there is no Room to doubt but it was the Urn of some considerable Roman Officer, and the best of the Kind that could be provided in their military Circumstances ; and that it was so seems plainly to appear from its Vicinity to the Roman Camp, the Engines that must have been employed to remove that vast Piece of Rock, and the Unlikeliness it should, or could, have ever been done by the Natives of the Country. But certainly the Design was to preserve those Remains from the Injuries of Rains and melting Snows, and to prevent their being profaned by the sacrilegious Hands of those they call Barbarians, for that reproachful Name, you know, they

II   T

gave to the People of almost all Nations but their own.

Give me leave to finish this Digression, which is grown already longer than I foresaw or intended.

As I returned the same Way from the Lowlands, I found the Officer, with his Party of working Soldiers, not far from the Stone, and asked him what was become of the Urn?

To this he answered, that he had intended to preserve it in the Condition I left it, till the Commander-in-Chief had seen it, as a Curiosity, but that it was not in his Power so to do; for soon after the Discovery was known to the Highlanders, they assembled from distant Parts, and having formed themselves into a Body, they carefully gathered up the Relics, and marched with them, in solemn Procession, to a new Place of Burial, and there discharged their Fire-arms over the Grave, as supposing the Deceased had been a military Officer.

You will believe the Recital of all this Ceremony led me to ask the Reason of such Homage done to the Ashes of a Person supposed to have been dead almost two thousand Years. I did so ; and the Officer, who was himself a Native of the Hills, told me that they (the Highlanders) firmly believe that if a dead Body should be known to lie above Ground, or be disinterred by Malice, or the Accidents of Torrents of Water, &c., and Care was not immediately taken to perform to it the proper Rites, then there would arise such Storms and Tempests as would destroy their Corn, blow away their Huts, and all Sorts of other Misfortunes would follow till that Duty was performed. You may here recollect what I told you so long ago, of the great Regard the Highlanders have for the Remains of their Dead ; but this Notion is entirely Roman.

But to return to my main Purpose.—In the Summer Seasons, five hundred of the Soldiers from the Barracks, and other Quarters about the Highlands, were employed in those Works in different Stations, by Detachments from the Regiments and Highland Companies.

The private Men were allowed Sixpence a Day, over and above their Pay as Soldiers: a Corporal had Eight-pence, and a Serjeant a Shilling; but this Extra Pay was only for working-Days, which were often interrupted by violent Storms of Wind and Rain, from the Heights and Hollows of the Mountains.

These Parties of Men were under the Command and Direction of proper Officers, who were all Subalterns, and received two Shillings and Sixpence *per Diem*, to defray their extraordinary Expense in building Huts: making necessary Provision for their Tables from Distant Parts; unavoidable though unwelcome Visits, and other Incidents arising from their wild Situation.

I should have told you before, that the non-commissioned Officers were constant and immediate Overseers of the Works.

The Standard Breadth of these Roads, as laid down at the first Projection, is sixteen Feet; but in some Parts, where there were no very expensive Difficulties, they are wider.

In those Places (as I have said before), they are carried on in straight Lines till some great Necessity has turned them out of the Way; the rest, which run along upon the Declivities of Hills, you know, must have their Circuits, Risings, and Descents accordingly.

To stop and take a general View of the Hills before you from an Eminence, in some Part where the Eye penetrates far within the void Spaces, the Roads would appear to you in a Kind of whimsical Disorder; and as those Parts of them that appear to you are of a very different Colour from the Heath that chiefly clothes the Country, they may, by that Contrast, be traced out to a considerable Distance.

Now, let us suppose that where you are, the Road is visible to you for a short Space, and is then broken off to the Sight by a Hollow or Winding among the Hills; beyond that Interruption, the eye catches a small Part on the Side of another Hill, and some again on the Ridge of it; in another Place, further off, the Road appears to run zigzag, in Angles, up a steep Declivity; in one Place, a short horizontal Line shows itself below, in another, the Marks of the Road seem to be almost even with the Clouds, &c.

It may here be objected, How can you see any Part of the flat Roof of a Building, when you are below? The Question would be just; but the Edges of the Roads on a Precipice, and the broken Parts of the Face of the Mountain behind, that has been wrought into to make Room for the Road,—these appear, and discover to them who are below the Line of which I have been speaking.

Thus the Eye catches one Part of the Road here, another there, in different Lengths and Positions; and, according to their Distance, they are diminished and rendered fainter and fainter, by the lineal and aërial Perspective, till they are entirely lost to Sight. And I need not tell you, that, as you pursue your Progress, the Scene changes to new Appearances.

The old Ways (for Roads I shall not call

them) consisted chiefly of stony Moors, Bogs, rugged, rapid Fords, Declivities of Hills, entangling Woods, and giddy Precipices. You will say this is a dreadful Catalogue to be read to him that is about to take a Highland Journey.

I have not mentioned the Valleys, for they are few in Number, far divided asunder, and generally the Roads through them were easily made.

My Purpose now is to give you some Account of the Nature of the particular Parts above-mentioned, and the Manner how this extraordinary Work has been executed; and this I shall do in the Order I have ranged them as above.

And first, the stony Moors. These are mostly Tracts of Ground of several Miles in Length, and often very high, with frequent lesser Risings and Descents, and having for Surface a Mixture of Stones and Heath. The Stones are fixed in the Earth, being very large and unequal, and generally are as deep in the

Ground as they appear above it; and where there are any Spaces between the Stones, there is a loose spongy Sward, perhaps not above five or six Inches deep, and incapable to produce any Thing but Heath, and all beneath it is hard Gravel or Rock.

I now begin to be apprehensive of your Memory, lest it should point out some Repetitions of Descriptions contained in my former Letters; but I have been thus particular, because I know the Extent of your Journeys, and that with you a Morass is called a Moor; yet Hills that are something of this Nature are called Moors in the North of England.

Here the Workmen first made room to fix their Instruments, and then, by Strength, and the Help of those two mechanic Powers, the Screw and the Lever, they raised out of their ancient Beds those massive Bodies, and then filling up the Cavities with Gravel, set them up, mostly end-ways, along the Sides of the Road, as Directions in Time of deep Snows, being some of them, as they now stand, eight or nine Feet high. They serve, likewise, as Memorials of the Skill and Labour requisite to the Performance of so difficult a Work.

In some particular Spots, where there was a proper Space beside the Stones, the Workmen dug Hollows, and, by undermining, dropped them in, where they lie buried so securely, as never more to retard the Traveller's Journey; but it was thought a moot Point, even where it was successful, whether any Time or Labour was saved by this Practice; for those Pits, for the most part, required to be made very deep and wide, and it could not be foreseen, without continual boring, whether there might not be Rock above the necessary Depth, which might be a Disappointment after great Labour.

The Roads on these Moors are now as smooth as Constitution-Hill, and I have gallopped on some of them for Miles together in great Tranquility; which was heightened by Reflection on my former Fatigue, when, for a great Part of the Way, I had been obliged to quit my Horse, it being too dangerous or impracticable to ride, and even hazardous to pass on Foot.

THE BOGS.

There are two Species of them, viz., Bogs, and those the Natives call Peat-Mosses, which yield them their Firing; many of the former are very large, and sometimes fill up the whole Space between the Feet of the Mountains. They are mostly not much, if any Thing, above the Level of the Sea; but I do not know that any Part of the Road is carried through them, or think it practicable; yet, as any Description of them may be new to you, I shall stop awhile to give you some Account of my *trotting* one of them, which is reckoned about a Mile over.

My Affairs engaging me to reside for some Time among the Hills, I resolved, and was preparing to make a Distant Visit; but was told that a Hill at the Foot of which I lived, was, in the Descent from it, exceeding steep and

stony ; I was therefore prevailed with to have
my Horses led a round-about Way, and to
meet me on the other Side.

In lieu of that difficult Way, I was to be
ferried over a Lake, and to traverse the Bog
above-mentioned, over which a Highlander
undertook to conduct me ; him I followed
close at the Heels, because I soon observed he
used a Step unlike to what he did upon firm
Ground, and which I could not presently
imitate ; and also that he chose his Way, here
and there, as if he knew where was the least
Danger, although, at the same Time, the
Surface of the Part we were going over,
seemed to me to be equally indifferent in
Respect to Safety and Danger.

Our Weight and the Spring of Motion, in
many Parts, caused a Shaking all round about
us, and the Compression made the Water rise
through the Sward, which was, in some Parts,
a kind of short flaggy Grass, and in others a
sort of Mossy Heath ; but wherever any
Rushes grew, I knew, by Experience of the

Peat-Mosses I had gone over before, that it was not far to the Bottom.

This Rising of Water made me conclude (for my Guide was not intelligible to me) that we had nothing but a Liquid under us, or, at most, something like a Quicksand, and that the Sward was only a little toughened by the Entwining of the Roots, and was supported, like Ice, only by Water, or something nearly as fluid.

I shall give you no Particulars of my Visit, further than that the Laird treated me in a very handsome and plentiful Manner, and, indeed, it was his Interest so to do ; but poor *Poke-Pudding* was so fatigued, and so apprehensive of Danger on the Bog, that he could not be persuaded to go back again the same Way.

THE MOSSES.

Of these I formerly gave you some superficial Account ; but now that I am about to let you know how the Roads were made through

them, I shall examine them to the Bottom.
When I first saw them, I imagined they were
formerly made when Woods were common in
the Hills ; but since, by several repeated
Laws, destroyed, to take away that Shelter
which assisted the Highlanders in their Depredations ;—I say, I have supposed the Leaves
of Trees were driven by Winds and lodged in
their Passage, from time to time, in those
Cavities till they were filled up. One Thing,
among others, that induced me to this Belief
is, that the muddy Substance of them is much
like the rotted Leaves in our Woods ; but,
since that Time, I have been told, that, when
one of them has been quite exhausted for
Fuel, it has grown again, and in the Course of
twenty Years, has been as fit to be dug for
firing as before. This I can believe, because
I have seen many small ones, far from any
Inhabitants, swelled above the Surface of the
Ground that lies all round about them, and
chiefly in the Middle, so as to become a Protuberance, and therefore by Strangers the less

suspected, though the deeper and more dangerous.

All beneath the Turf is a spongy Earth interwoven with a slender, fibrous Vegetable, something like the smallest Roots of a Shrub, and these a little toughen it, and contribute to the making it good Fuel; but, when they are quite, or near dug out, the Pit is generally almost filled with Water. This, I suppose, arises from Springs, which may, for aught I know, have been the first Occasion of these Mosses, which are very deceitful, especially to those who are not accustomed to them, being mostly covered with Heath, like the rest of the Country, and, in time of Rains, become soft, and sometimes impassable on Foot.

Now that I have no further Occasion for any Distinction, I shall call every soft Place a Bog, except there be Occasion sometimes to vary the Phrase.

When one of these Bogs has crossed the Way on a stony Moor, there the loose Ground has been dug out down to the Gravel, or Rock,

and the Hollow filled up in the Manner following, viz.

First with a Layer of large Stones, then a
smaller Size, to fill up the Gaps and raise the
Causeway higher; and, lastly, two, three, or
more Feet of Gravel, to fill up the Interstices
of the small Stones, and form a smooth and
binding Surface. This Part of the Road has
a Bank on each Side, to separate it from a
Ditch, which is made withoutside to receive
the Water from the Bog, and, if the Ground
will allow it, to convey it by a Trench to a
Slope, and thereby in some measure drain it.

In a rocky Way, where no loose Stones
were to be found, if a Bog intervened, and
Trees could be had at any portable Distance,
the Road has been made solid by Timber and
Fascines, crowned with Gravel, dug out of the
Side of some Hill.

This is durable; for the Faggots and Trees,
lying continually in the Moisture of the Bog,
will, instead of decaying, become extremely
hard, as has been observed of Trees that have

been plunged into those Sloughs, and lain there, in all Probability, for many Ages. This Causeway has likewise a Bank and a Ditch for the Purpose above-mentioned.

There is one Bog I passed through (literally speaking), which is upon the Declivity of a Hill ; there the Mud has been dug away for a proper Space, and thrown upon the Bog on either Side, and a Passage made at the Foot of a Hill for the Water to run down into a large Cavity, insomuch, that, by continual draining, I rode, as it were, in a very shallow Rivulet running down the Hill upon a Rock (which was made smooth by the Workmen), with the Sides of the Bog high above me on both Sides, like one of the Hollow Ways in England.

I must desire you will consider, that the foregoing Descriptions, as well as these that are to follow, are, and will be, only Specimens of the Work ; for it would be almost without End to give you all the Particulars of so various and extensive a Performance.

FORDS.

No Remedy but Bridges has been found for the Inconveniences and Hazards of these rugged and rapid Passages; for, when some of them, in the Beginning, were cleared from the large, loose Stones, the next Inundation brought down others in their Room, which else would have been stopped by the Way, and some of those were of a much larger Size than the Stones that had been removed.

This was the Case (among others) of a small River, which, however, was exceedingly dangerous to ford, and for that reason the first Bridge was ordered to be built over it; but it gave me a lively Idea how short is human Foresight, especially in new Projects and untried Undertakings.

The Spring of the Arch was founded upon Rocks, and it was elevated much above the highest Water that had ever been known by the Country-People; yet, some time after it was finished, there happened a sudden Torrent

from the Mountains, which brought down
Trees and Pieces of Rocks; and, by its being
placed too near the Issue of Water from between two Hills, though firmly built with
Stone, it was cropt off, not far beneath the
Crown of the Arch, as if it had neither Weight
nor Solidity.

DECLIVITIES.

By these I mean the sloping Sides of the
Hills whereon the new Roads are made.

The former Ways along those Slopes were
only Paths worn by the Feet of the Highlanders and their little Garrons. They ran
along upwards and downwards, one above
another, in such a manner as was found most
convenient at the first tracing them out: this,
I think, I have observed to you formerly.

To these narrow Paths the Passenger was
confined (for there is seldom any Choice of
the Way you would take in the Highlands) by
the Impassability of the Hollows at the Feet of
the Mountains; because those Spaces, in some

Parts, are filled up with deep Bogs, or fallen Rocks, of which last I have seen many as big as a middling-House; and, looking up, have observed others, at an exceeding Height, in some Measure parted from the main Rock, and threatening the Crush of some of those below. In other Parts there are Lakes beneath, and sometimes, where there are none, it was only by these Paths you could ascend the Hills, still proceeding round the Sides of them from one to another.

There the new Roads have been carried on in more regular Curves than the old Paths, and are dug into the Hills, which are sloped away above them; and where any Rocks have occurred in the Performance, they have been bored and blown away with Gunpowder.

Above the Road are Trenches made to receive Rains, melting Snows, and Springs, which last are in many Places continually issuing out of the Sides of the Hills, being draining away from large Waters collected in Lakes, and other Cavities, above in the Mountains.

From the above-mentioned Trenches are proper Channels made to convey the Water down the Hills ; these are secured, by firm Pavement, from being gulled by the Stream : and in Places that required it, there are Stone Walls built behind the Road to prevent the Fall of Earth or Stones from the broken Part of the Declivity.

WOODS.

These are not only rare in the Way of the New Roads, but I have formerly given you some Description of the Inconvenience and Danger of one of them, and therefore I shall only add, in this Place, that the Trees, for the necessary Space, have been cut down and grubbed up; their fibrous Roots, that ran about upon the Surface, destroyed ; the boggy Part removed ; the Rock smoothed, and the Crannies firmly filled up ; and all this in such a Manner as to make of it a very commodious Road.

STEEP ASCENTS.

As the Heights, for the most Part, are attained, as I have been saying, by going round the Sides of the Hills from one to another, the exceeding steep Ascents are not very common in the ordinary Passages ; but where they are, the Inconvenience and Difficulties of them have been removed.

I shall only instance in one, which, indeed, is confessed to be the worst of them all. This is the Coriarack Mountain, before mentioned, which rises in the Way that leads from Dalwhinny to Fort-Augustus. It is above a Quarter of a Mile of perpendicular Height, and was passed by few besides the Soldiery when the Garrisons were changed, as being the nearest Way from one of the Barracks to another ; and had it not been for the Conveniency of that Communication, this Part of the new Roads had never been thought of.

This Mountain is so near the Perpendicular in some Parts, that it was doubtful whether the Passenger, after great Labour, should get upwards, or return much quicker, than he advanced.

The Road over it, not to mention much Roughness (which I believe, you have had enough of by this Time, and are likely to have more), is carried on upon the South Declivity of the Hill, by seventeen Traverses, like the Course of a Ship when she is turning to Windward, by Angles still advancing higher and higher; yet little of it is to be seen below, by Reason of Flats, Hollows, and Windings that intercept the Sight; and nothing could give you a general View of it, unless one could be supposed to be placed high above the Mountain in the Air   This is much unlike your Hills in the South, that, in some convenient Situation of the Eye, are seen in one continued smooth Slope from the Bottom to the Top.

Each of the above-mentioned Angles is about seventy or eighty Yards in Length, except in a few Places where the Hill would not admit of all that Extent.

These Traverses upward, and the Turnings of their Extremities, are supported on the Outside of the Road by Stone Walls, from ten to fifteen Feet in Height.

Thus that steep Ascent, which was so difficult to be attained, even by the Foot-Passenger, is rendered everywhere more easy for Wheel-carriages than Highgate Hill.

On the North-Side of this Mountain, at a Place named Snugburgh from its Situation, there is a narrow Pass between two exceeding high and steep Hills. These are joined together by two Arches, supported by Walls, to take off the Sharpness of the short Descent, which otherwise could not have been practicable for the lightest Wheel-carriage whatever, for it was difficult even for Horse or Man.

PRECIPICES.

I shall say nothing in this Place of such of them as are any Thing tolerable to the Mind, in passing them over, though a false Step might render them fatal, as there would be no stopping till dashed against the Rocks. I shall only mention two that are the most terrible, which I have gone over several Times, but always occasionally, not as the shortest Way, or by Choice, but to avoid extensive Bogs, or swelling Waters in Time of Rain, which I thought more dangerous in the other Way.

One of these Precipices is on the North Side of the Murray Frith, where no Roads have been made ; the other is on a Mountain southward of this Town.

Both these, as I have said above, were useful upon Occasion ; but the latter is now rendered unnecessary, as the old round-about Way is made smooth, and Bridges built over the dangerous Waters, and therefore nothing has been done to this Precipice ; nor, indeed, was it thought practicable to widen the Path, by Reason of the Steepness of the Side of the Hill that rises above it.

I think the ordinary Proverb was never more manifestly verified than it now is, in these two several Ways : viz.—" That the farthest

Way about," &c. Yet, I make no Doubt, the Generality of the Highlanders will prefer the Precipice to the Gravel of the Road and a greater Number of Steps.

Not far from this steep Place I once baited my Horses with Oats, carried with me, and laid upon the Snow in the Month of July; and, indeed, it is there (instead of Rain) Snow or Sleet all the Year round.

Thus far I have, chiefly in general Terms, described the Difficulties that attended the making new Roads, and the Methods taken to surmount them, which was all I at first intended; but as some of the greatest Obstacles, which yet remain undescribed, were met with in the Way between this Town and Fort-William, I shall, previous to any account of them, endeavour to give you some Idea of this Passage between the Mountains, wherein lies no small Part of the Roads; and this I shall the rather do, because that Hollow, for Length and Figure, is unlike any Thing of the Kind I have seen in other Parts of the Highlands;

and I hope to accomplish all I have to say of it before I leave this Town, being very shortly to make a Northern Progress among the Hills, wherein I shall find none of those Conveniences we now have on this Side the Murray Frith.

This Opening would be a surprising Prospect to such as never have seen a high Country, being a Mixture of Mountains, Waters, Heath, Rocks, Precipices, and scattered Trees; and that for so long an Extent, in which the Eye is confined within the Space; and, therefore, if I should pretend to give you a full Idea of it, I should put myself in the Place of one that has had a strange preposterous Dream, and, because it has made a strong Impression on him, he fondly thinks he can convey it to others in the same Likeness as it remains painted on his Memory; and, in the End, wonders at the Coldness with which it was received.

This Chasm begins about four Miles West of Inverness, and, running across the Island,

divides the northern from the southern Highlands. It is chiefly taken up by Lakes,
bounded on both Sides by high Mountains,
which almost everywhere (being very steep at
the Feet) run down exceedingly deep into the
Water. The first of the Lakes, beginning
from the East, is Loch-Ness, which I have
formerly mentioned. It lies in a Line along
the Middle of it, as direct as an artificial Canal.
This I have observed myself, from a rising
Ground at the East End, by directing a small
Telescope to Fort-Augustus, at the other
Extreme.

I have said it is straight by the Middle only,
because the Sides are irregular, being so made
by the jutting of the Feet of the Hills into the
Water on either Side, as well as by the Spaces
between them ; and the various Breadths of
different Parts of the Lake.

The Depth, the Nature of the Water, and
the remarkable Cataracts on the South Side,
have been occasionally mentioned in former
Letters ; and I think I have told you, it is one-

and-twenty Scots Miles in Length, and from one to near two Miles in Breadth.

It has hardly any perceptible Current, notwithstanding it receives a vast Conflux of Waters from the bordering Mountains, by Rivers and Rivulets that discharge themselves into it. Yet all the Water that visibly runs from it in the greatest Rains, is limited in its Course by the River Ness, by which it has its Issue into the Sea, and that River is not, in some Places, above twenty Yards wide; and therefore I think the greatest Part of the Superfluity must be drained away by subterraneous Passages.

I have told you long ago, that it never freezes in the calmest and severest Frost; and by its Depth (being in some Parts 360 Yards), and by its Breadth, and the violent Winds that pass through the Opening, it often has a Swell not much inferior to the Ocean.

In several Parts on the Sides of the Lake, you see Rocks of a Kind of coarse black Marble, and I think as hard as the best; these rise to a considerable Height, which never, till lately, were trod by human Foot ; for the old Way made a considerable Circuit from this Lake, and did not come to it but at the West End. In other Places are Woods upon the steep Declivities, which serve to abate the Deformity of those Parts ;—I say abate, for the Trees being, as I said above, confusedly scattered one above another, they do not hide them. All the rest is Heath and Rock.

Some Time ago there was a Vessel, of about five-and-twenty or thirty Tons Burden, built at the East End of this Lake, and called the Highland Galley.

She carries six or eight Pattereroes, and is employed to transport Men, Provision, and Baggage to Fort-Augustus, at the other End of the Lake.

The Master has an Appointment from the Government, to navigate this Vessel, and to keep her in Repair.

When she made her first Trip she was mightily adorned with Colours, and fired her

Guns several Times, which was a strange Sight to the Highlanders, who had never seen the like before;—at least, on that inland Lake.

For my own Part, I was not less amused with the Sight of a good Number of Highland-Men and Women upon the Highest Part of a Mountain over-against us;—I mean the highest that appeared to our View.

These People, I suppose, were brought to the Precipice, from some Flat behind, by the Report of the Guns (for even a single Voice is understood at an incredible Height) ; and, as they stood, they appeared to the naked Eye not to be a Foot high in Stature ; but, by the Assistance of a pretty long Glass, I could plainly see their Surprise and Admiration. And I must confess I wondered not much less to see so many People on such a monstrous Height, who could not inhabit there in Winter, till I reflected it was the Time of the Year for them to go up to their Sheelings. And I was told that they, like us, were not far from a spacious Lake, though in that elevated Situation.

I need not trouble you with a Description of
the other two Waters and their Boundaries,
there being but little Difference between them
and the former; only here the old Ways, such
as they were, ran along upon the Sides of the
Hills, which were in a great Measure rocky
Precipices, and that these Lakes are not quite
so wide, and incline a little more to the Southward of the West than the other.

The next Lake to Loch-Ness (which, as I
have said, is twenty-one Miles in Length) is Loch
Oich; this is four Miles long; and Loch Lochy,
the last of the three, is nine, in all thirty-four
Miles, Part of the forty-eight, which is the
whole Length of the Opening, and at the End
thereof is Fort-William, on the west Coast, to
which the Sea flows, as it does likewise to Inverness on the East. Thus the whole Extent
of Ground, between Sea and Sea, is fourteen
Miles.

Here I must stop a little to acquaint you
with a Spot of Ground which I take to be
something remarkable. This I had passed

over several Times without observing any Thing extraordinary in it, and, perhaps, should never have taken Notice of it, if it had not been pointed out to me by one of the Natives.

About the Middle of the Neck of Land that divides the Lakes Oich and Lochy (which is but one Mile), not far from the Centre of the Opening, there descends from the Hills, on the South Side, a Bourn, or Rivulet, which, as it falls upon the Plain, divides into two Streams without any visible Ridge to part them; and one of them runs through the Lakes Oich and Ness into the East Sea, and the other takes the quite contrary Course, and passes through Loch Lochy into the Western Ocean.

This, and the short Space of Land above-mentioned, have given Birth to several Projects for making a navigable Communication across the Island, not only to divide effectually the Highlands by the Middle, but to save the tedious, costly, and hazardous Voyages through

St. George's Channel, or otherwise round by the Isles of Orkney.

This Spot, the Projectors say, is a Level between the two Seas, pointed out as it were by the Hand of Nature, and they pretend the Space of Land to be cut through is practicable.

But it would be an incredible Expense to cut fourteen navigable Miles in so rocky a Country, and there is yet a stronger Objection, which is, that the whole Opening lies in so direct a Line, and the Mountains that bound it are so high, the Wind is confined in its Passage, as it were, in the Nozle of a pair of Bellows; so that, let it blow from what Quarter it will without the Opening, it never varies much from East or West within.

This would render the Navigation so precarious that hardly anybody would venture on it, not to mention the violent flurries of Wind that rush upon the Lakes by Squalls from the Spaces between the Hills, and also the rocky Shores, want of Harbour and Anchorage; and,

II.   X

perhaps, there might appear other unforeseen Inconveniences and Dangers, if it were possible the Work could be completed.

There are three Garrisons in this Line, which reaches from East to West, viz. Fort-George, at Inverness, Fort-Augustus, at Killichumen, and Fort-William, in Lochaber, and every one of them pretty equally distant from one another; and the Line might be made yet more effectual by Redoubts, at proper Distances between them, to prevent the sudden joining of Numbers ill affected to the Government.

Having given you some Account of this Chasm, I shall, in the next Place, say something of the Road that lies quite through it, together with some Difficulties that attended the Work, of which all that Part which runs along near the Edges of the Lakes is on the South Side; but, as I have already bestowed so many Words upon Subjects partly like this, I shall confine myself to very few Particulars; and of the rest, which may come under those former Descriptions, I need say no more, if I have been intelligible.

I shall begin with that Road which goes along above Loch-Ness.

This is entirely new, as I have hinted before; and, indeed, I might say the same of every Part; but I mean there was no Way at all along the Edge of this Lake till this Part of the Road was made.

It is, good Part of it, made out of Rocks; but, among them all, I shall mention but one, which is of a great Length, and, as I have said before, as hard as Marble.

There the Miners hung by Ropes from the Precipice over the Water (like Shakespear's Gatherers of Samphire from Dover Cliffs) to bore the Stone, in order to blow away a necessary Part from the Face of it, and the rest likewise was chiefly done by Gunpowder; but, when any Part was fit to be left as it was, being flat and smooth, it was brought to a Roughness proper for a Stay to the Feet; and, in this Part, and all the rest of the Road,

where the Precipices were like to give Horror
or Uneasiness to such as might pass over them
in Carriages, though at a good Distance from
them, they are secured to the Lake-side by
Walls, either left in the Working, or built up
with Stone, to a Height proportioned to the
Occasion.

Now, for the Space of twelve Miles, it is an
even Terrace in every Part, from whence the
Lake may be seen from End to End, and from
whence the romantic Prospect of the rugged
Mountains would, I dare say, for its Novelty,
be more entertaining to you than it is to me;
—I say, it might be agreeable to you, who,
not having these hideous Productions of Nature
near you, wantonly procure even bad Imitations
of them, in little artificial Rocks and diminutive
Cataracts of Water. But as some Painters
travel to Italy, in order to study or copy the
most admirable Performances of the great
Masters, for their own Instruction, so I would
advise your Artisans, in that Way, to visit this
Country for their better Information.

The next Part of this Road which I am about to speak of, is that which lies along the Side of the Hills, arising from the Edge of Loch-Oich.

The Dangers of this Part of the old Way began at the Top of a steep Ascent, of about fifty or sixty Yards from the little Plain that parts this Lake and Loch-Ness; and, not far from the Summit, is a Part they call the *Maiden's-Leap*, of which they tell a strange romantic Story, not worth the Remembrance. There the Rocks project over the Lake, and the Path was so rugged and narrow that the Highlanders were obliged, for their Safety, to hold by the Rocks and Shrubs as they passed, with the Prospect of Death beneath them.

This was not the only dangerous Part; but for three Miles together, Part of the Four (which I have said is the Length of this Lake), it was nowhere safe, and in many Places more difficult, and as dangerous, as at the Entrance; for the Rocks were so steep and uneven, that the Passenger was obliged to creep on his Hands and Knees.

These Precipices were so formidable to some that they chose rather to cross the Plain above-mentioned, and wade a River on the opposite Side of the Opening, which by others was thought more hazardous in its Kind than the Way which their Fear excited them to avoid; and when they had passed that Water, they had a wide Circuit to make among steep and rugged Hills, before they could get again into the Way they were to go.

The last Part of the Road along the Lakes (as I have divided it into three) runs along on the Declivities of Loch-Lochy, and reaches the whole Length of that Lake, which, as I have said before, is nine Miles.

This was much of the same Nature as the last, exceeding steep, with Rocks in several Places hanging over the Water, and required a great Quantity of Gunpowder; but, both this and the other two are now as commodious as any other of the Roads in the Highlands, which everywhere (bating Ups and Downs) are equal in Goodness to the best in England.

I shall say nothing of the Way from the End of this Lake to Fort-William, any more than I have done of the Road from Inverness to Loch-Ness, or the Spaces between the Lakes, because they may be comprehended in the ordinary Difficulties already described.

But I might acquaint you with many other Obstacles which were thought, at first, to be insurmountable; such as Slock-Moach, between Ruthven and Inverness, the rocky Pass of Killicranky, in Athol, between Dunkeld and the Blair, &c.

I shall only say, that I have formerly given you some Description of the first, but without a Name, in the Account of an Incursion I made to the Hills from Inverness; but, both this and the other, which were very bad, are now made easily passable.

The Name of Slock-Moach is interpreted by the Natives, a *Den of Hogs*, having been, as they say it was formerly, a noted Harbour for Thieves; who, in Numbers, lay in wait within that narrow and deep Cavity, to commit their Depredations upon Cattle and Passengers. I suppose this Name was given to it when Swine were held in Abomination among the Highlanders.

The first Design of removing a vast fallen Piece of a Rock was entertained by the Country People with great Derision, of which I saw one Instance myself.

A very old wrinkled Highland Woman, upon such an Occasion, standing over-against me, when the Soldiers were fixing their Engines, seemed to sneer at it, and said something to an Officer of one of the Highland Companies. I imagined she was making a Jest of the Undertaking, and asked the Officer what she said. "I will tell you her Words," said he:

"What are the Fools a-doing? That Stone will lie there for ever, for all them." But when she saw that vast Bulk begin to rise, though by slow Degrees, she set up a hideous Irish Yell, took to her Heels, ran up the Side of a Hill just by, like a young Girl, and never looked behind her while she was within our Sight. I make no Doubt she thought it was Magic, and the Workmen Warlocks.

This, indeed, was the Effect of an old Woman's Ignorance and Superstition; but a Gentleman, esteemed for his good Understanding, when he had seen the Experiment of the first Rock above Loch-Ness, said to the Officer that directed the Work, "When first I heard of this Undertaking, I was strangely scandalised to think how shamefully you would come off; but now I am convinced there is nothing can stand before you and Gunpowder."

Notwithstanding there may be no Remains of my former Letters, I believe your Memory may help you to reflect what wretched Lodging there was in the Highlands when those Epistles were written. This Evil is now remedied, as far as could be done; and in that

Road, where there were none but Huts of
Turf for a hundred Miles together, there
now are Houses with Chimneys, built with
Stone and Lime, and ten or twelve Miles
distance one from another; and though they
are not large, yet are they well enough
adapted to the Occasion of Travellers, who
are seldom many at a Time in that Country.
But I would not be understood that there is
any better Accommodation than before, besides warm Lodging.   Another Thing is,
there are Pillars set up at the End of every
five Miles, mostly upon Eminences, which
may not only amuse the Passenger and
lessen the Tediousness of the Way, but prevent his being deceived in Point of Time, in
Rain, Snow, Drift, or approaching Night.

But the last, and I think, the greatest Conveniency, is the Bridges, which prevent the
Dangers of the terrible Fords.

Of these I shall say but little, because to
you they are no Novelty.   They are forty in
Number; some of them single Arches, of forty

or fifty Feet diameter, mostly founded upon
Rocks; others are composed of two; one of
three, and one of five, Arches. This last is
over the Tay, and is the only Bridge upon that
wild River, as has been said before. It is built
with Astler-Stone, and is 370 Feet in Length.
The middle arch is sixty Feet diameter, and it
bears the following Inscription, made Latin
from English, as I have been told, by Dr.
Friend, Master of Westminster School :—

Mirare
Viam hanc Militarem
Ultra Romanos Terminos
M. Passuum CCL. *hac illac extensam*
Tesquis et Paludibus insultantem
Per Rupes Montesque patefactam
Et indignanti Tavo
Ut cernis instratam
Opus hoc arduum suâ solertiâ
Et decennali Militum Operâ
Anno Ær. Christæ 1733, *perfecit* G. Wade.
Copiarum in Scotia *Præfectus.*
Ecce quantum valeant
Regia Georgii *Secundi Auspicia.*

The Objections made to these new Roads
and Bridges, by some in the several Degrees

of *Condition* among the Highlanders, are in Part as follow: viz.—

I. Those Chiefs and other Gentlemen complain, that thereby an easy Passage is opened into their Country for Strangers, who, in Time, by their Suggestions of Liberty, will destroy or weaken that Attachment of their Vassals which it is so necessary for them to support and preserve.

That their Fastnesses being laid open, they are deprived of that Security from Invasion which they formerly enjoyed.

That the Bridges, in particular, will render the ordinary People effeminate, and less fit to pass the Waters in other Places where there are none.

And there is a pecuniary Reason concealed, relating to some foreign Courts, which to you I need not explain.

II. The middling Order say the Roads are to them an Inconvenience, instead of being useful, as they have turned them out of their old Ways; for their Horses being never shod, the Gravel would soon whet away their Hoofs, so as to render them unserviceable : whereas the Rocks and Moor-Stones, though together they make a rough Way, yet, considered separately, they are generally pretty smooth on the Surface where they tread, and the Heath is always easy to their Feet. To this I have been inconsiderately asked, " Why then do they not shoe their Horses ?"

This Question is easily put, and costs nothing but a few various Sounds. But where is the Iron, the Forge, the Farrier, the People within a reasonable Distance to maintain him ? And lastly, where is the principal Requisite— Money ?

III. The lowest Class, who, many of them, at some Times cannot compass a Pair of Shoes for themselves, they allege, that the Gravel is intolerable to their naked Feet ; and the Complaint has extended to their thin *Brogues.*

It is true they do sometimes, for these Reasons, go without the Road, and ride or walk in very incommodious Ways. This has induced some of our Countrymen, especially such as have been at Minorca (where Roads of this Kind have likewise been made), to accuse the Highlanders of Spanish Obstinacy, in refusing to make Use of so great a Conveniency, purely because it is a Novelty introduced by the English. But why do the black Cattle do the same Thing? Certainly for the Ease of their Feet.

Nor can I believe that either Highlanders or Spaniards are such Fools as to deprive themselves of any considerable Benefit upon a Principle so ridiculous. But I fear it is our own Pride that suggests such contemptuous Thoughts of Strangers. I have seen a great deal of it, and have often thought of Lochart's Accusation, in a Book that goes under the Name of his Memoirs, where he says—"'The English despise all Nations but their own, for which all the World hates them;" or to that Purpose. But whether his Observation be just or not, it is in the Breast of every one to determine for himself. For my own Part, ever since I have known the Highlands, I never doubted but the Natives had their Share of natural Understanding with the rest of Mankind.

Notwithstanding I have finished my Account of the Roads, which was all I at first intended, and although this Letter is almost grown into a Volume, yet, like other great Talkers, I cannot conclude it with Satisfaction to myself till I have told my Tale quite out.

Fort-Augustus, at Killichumen, is not only near the Middle of the Opening of which I have said so much, but is likewise reckoned to be the most centrical Point of the habitable Part of the Highlands.

The old Barrack was built in the Year 1716; I need not tell you upon what Occasion. It stands upon a rising Ground, at about two or three hundred Yards Distance from the Head of Loch-Ness, and the new Fort is just upon the Border of that Water. Before there was any great Progress made in building that Fortress, it was proposed to make a covered

Way of Communication between both, and
that it should be the principal Garrison of the
Highlands, and the Residence of a Governor,
who was likewise to command the other two
in that Line, viz., Fort-George, at Inverness,
and Fort-William, in Lochaber, which two
last were to be under the Command of Lieu-
tenant-Governors; this was the Military
Scheme. But, besides there was a civil
Project on Foot, which was to build a Town
after the English Manner, and procure for it
all the Privileges and Immunities of a royal
borough in Scotland.

These Advantages, it was said, would invite
Inhabitants to settle there, not only from the
Lowlands, but even from England, and make
it the principal Mart of the Highlands, by
which Means the Natives would be drawn
thither as to the Centre; and by accustoming
themselves to Strangers, grow desirous of a
more commodious Way of living than their
own, and be enabled by Traffic to maintain it.
And thus (it was said) they would be weaned

from their barbarous Customs. But surely this Scheme was as *wild* as the Highlanders whom it was proposed to *tame* by it; yet it was entertained for some Months with Fondness. But Anger blinds and deceives the Judgment by the promised Sweets of Revenge, as Avarice does by the pleasing Thoughts of Gain, though unlawful. And I think I may premise to what I am about to say, that successful Revenge is wicked; but an impotent Desire of it is not only wicked, but ridiculous. Perhaps you will say I moralize, and you do not yet see the Application; but you will hardly believe that this Utopian Town had no other Foundation than a Pique against two or three of the Magistrates of Inverness, for whose Transgression their Town was to be humbled by this Contrivance.

I shall wave all Considerations of the Intent to Punish a whole Community upon a Prejudice taken against two or three of them, and only show you how improbable the Success of such an Undertaking would have been: and

II.   Y

if it had been likely, how distant the Prospect of the pleasure proposed by it.

A Town of any Manner of Consideration would take up all, or most Part of the Country (for so the Highlanders call every arable Flat that lies between the Mountains); and the Place is not above five-and-twenty Miles (including the Lake) from Inverness, which is a Sea-port Town, and well situated for Improvement of foreign Trade and home Manufactures. But the inner Parts of the Highlands will not admit even of Manu-factories; for the Inhabitants are few that can be spared from their Farms, which, though they are but small, are absolutely necessary to Life; and they are scattered among the Hills at great Distances, and the habitable Spaces are generally not large enough to contain any considerable Number of People, or the whole Country within reach all round about, sufficient to furnish them with necessary Provisions. And lastly, Strangers will not be admitted among the Clans.

By the Way, I have been told the Welsh are not much less averse than the Highlanders to any Settlement of Strangers among them, though extremely hospitable to Visitants, and such as have some temporary Business to transact in their Country.—But to return to my Purpose.

As to the Corn received by the Lairds from their Tenants, as Rent in Kind, and the Cattle, when marketable, the first has always been sold by Contract to Lowland Merchants, and the Cattle are driven to such Fairs and Markets of the Low Country as are nearest, or otherwise commodious or beneficial to the Drovers and their Employers. And therefore there is no Manner of Likelihood that either the one or the other should be brought to any Highland Market.

I have told you in a former Letter, what *Kinds* and *Quantities* of Merchandise were usually brought by the Highlanders, to the Fairs at Inverness.

It was a supposition very extraordinary to

suppose, that any Lowlanders who could subsist in another Place, would shut themselves up in such a Prison, without any reasonabler Prospect of Advantage ; and I verily believe there is not an Englishman, when he knew the Country, but would think of a Settlement there with more Horror than any Russian would do of Banishment to Siberia.

But lastly, if it were possible to suppose there were none of these Obstacles, how long a Time must have been required to People this new Colony, and to render it capable to rival an old established Town like Inverness : I need not recite the Proverb of the growing Grass ; it is too obvious.

Yet if the Inhabitants of the new Settlement proposed, could have lived upon Air, I verily believe they would have been fed with better Diet than at Montpelier.

Thus am I providing Work for myself, but am not so sure it will be Entertainment to you ; for now I have happened to speak of the Healthfulness of the Spot, I must tell you whereupon I found my Opinion.

The Officers and Soldiers garrisoned in that Barrack, for many Successions have found it to be so ; and several of them who were fallen into a valetudinary State in other Parts, have there recovered their Health in a short Time. Among other Instances, I shall give you only one, which I thought almost a Miracle.

A certain Officer of the Army, when in London, was advised by his Physicians to go into the Country for better Air, as you know is customary with them, when mere shame deters them from taking further Fees ; and likewise that the Patient may be hid under ground, out of the Reach of all reflecting observation within the Circuit of their Practice. But the Corps he belonged to being then quartered in the Highlands, he resolved by gentle Journeys, to endeavour to reach it, but expected (as he told me) nothing but Death by the Way ; however he came to that Place one Evening, unknown to me,

though I was then in the Barrack, and the
next Morning early I saw upon the Parade,
a Stranger, which is there an unusual Sight.
He was in a deep Consumption, sadly ema-
ciated, and with Despair in his Countenance,
surveying the Tops of the Mountains. I
went to him; and after a few Words of
Welcome, &c., his uttermost Thoughts became
audible in a Moment. " Lord ! " says he, " to
what a Place am I come ?   There can nothing
but Death be expected here."   I own I had
conceived a good Opinion of that Part of the
Country, and, therefore, as well as in common
Complaisance, should in Course have given
him some Encouragement : but I do not know
how it was ; I happened at that Instant to be,
as it were, inspired with a Confidence not
ordinary with me, and told him peremptorily
and positively the Country would cure him;
and repeated several Times, as if I knew it
would be so.   How ready is Hope with
her Assistance !   Immediately I observed his
Features to clear up, like the Day, when

the Sun begins to peep over the Edge of a Cloud.

To be short : he mended daily in his Health, grew perfectly well in a little Time, obtained Leave to return to England, and soon after married a Woman with a considerable Fortune.

I know so well your Opinion of the Doctor's Skill, that, if I should tell you there was not a Physician in the Country, you would say it was that very Want which made the Air so healthy, and was the Cause of that wonderful Cure.

This poor but wholesome Spot reminds me of a Quack that mounted a Stage in Westminster, but was there very unsuccessful in the Sale of his Packets. At the End of his Harangue he told his Mob-Audience (among whom, being but a Boy, myself was one), that he should immediately truss up his Baggage and be gone, because he found they had no Occasion for Physic ; "For," says he, " you live in an Air so healthy, that where one of you dies, there are twenty that run away." But to proceed to a Conclusion, which I foresee is not far off.

At Fort-William, which is not above three or four and twenty Miles Westward of Fort-Augustus, I have heard the People talk as familiarly of a Shower (as they call it) of nine or ten Weeks, as they would do of any Thing else that was not out of the ordinary Course; but the Clouds that are brought over-Sea by the Westerly Winds are there attracted and broke by the exceedingly high Mountains, and mostly exhausted before they reach the middle of the Highlands at Fort-Augustus; and nothing has been more common with us about Inverness, on the East Coast, than to ride or walk to recreate ourselves in Sunshine, when we could clearly see through the Opening, for Weeks together, the west side of the Island involved in thick Clouds. This was often the Occasion of a *good-natured* triumph with us to observe what a *Pickle* our opposite Neighbours were in ;

but I am told the Difference in that Particular, between the East and Western Part of England, near the Coast, is much the same in Proportion to the Height of the Hills.

I have but one Thing more to take Notice of in relation to the Spot of which I have been so long speaking, and that is, I have been sometimes vexed with a little Plague (if I may use the Expression), but do not you think I am too grave upon the Subject ; there are great Swarms of little Flies which the Natives call *Malhoulakins : Houlack*, they tell me, signifies, in the Country Language, a *Fly*, and *Houlakin* is the Diminutive of that Name. These are so very small, that, separately, they are but just perceptible and that is all ; and, being of a blackish Colour, when a Number of them settle upon the Skin, they make it look as if it was dirty ; there they soon bore with their little Augers into the Pores, and change the Face from black to red.

They are only troublesome (I should say intolerable) in Summer, when there is a profound Calm; for the least Breath of Wind immediately disperses them; and the only Refuge from them is the House, into which I never knew them to enter. Sometimes, when I have been talking to any one, I have (though with the utmost Self-denial) endured their Stings to watch his Face, and see how long they would suffer him to be quiet; but in three or four Seconds, he has slapped his Hand upon his Face, and in great Wrath cursed the little Vermin: but I have found the same Torment in some other Parts of the Highlands where Woods were at no great Distance.

Here I might say, if it did not something savour of a Pun, that I have related to you the most *minute* Circumstances of this long and straight *Opening* of the Mountains.

As my former Letters relating to this Country were the Effects of your Choice, I could then apologize for them with a tolerable Grace; but now that I have obtruded myself upon you, without so much as asking your

Consent, or giving you the least Notice, I have divested myself of that Advantage, and therefore shall I take the quite contrary Course, and boldly justify myself in what I have done. You know there is no other Rule to judge of the Quality of many Things but by Comparison; and this being of their Nature, I do affirm with the last Confidence (for I have not been here so long for Nothing), that the following Subjects are inferior to mine either for Information or Entertainment, viz.

1st. The Genealogy of a particular family, in which but very few others are interested; and, by the bye, for you know I am apt to digress, it must be great Good-nature and Christian Charity to suppose it impossible that any one of the *auxiliary Sex* should step out of the Way to the *Aid* of some other in the many Successions of five hundred Years; and, if that should happen, I would know what *Relation* there then is between him that boasts of his Ancestry and the Founder of the Family; certainly none but the Estate; and if that which is the main Prop should fail, the high Family would soon tumble from its Eminence; but this is but very little of that just Ridicule that attends this kind of Vanity.

We are told that none are Gentlemen among the Chinese, but such as have rendered themselves worthy of the Title.

2dly. Tedious Collections of the Sentiments of great Numbers of Authors upon Subjects that, in all Likelihood, had never any Being—but this is a Parade of Reading.

3dly. Trifling Antiquities, hunted out of their mouldy Recesses, which serve to no other Purpose but to expose the injudicious Searcher.

4thly. Tiresome Criticisms upon a single Word, when it is not of the least Consequence whether there is, or ever was, any such Sound.

5thly. Dissertations upon Butterflies, which would take up almost as much Time in the Reading as the whole Life of that Insect— *cum multis aliis.*

This small Scrap of Latin has escaped me, and I think it is the only *Air* of Learning, as they call it, that I have given to any of my Letters, from the Beginning to this Time, and even now I might have expressed the Sense of it in homely English with as few Words, and a Sound as agreeable to the Ear: but some are as fond of larding with Latin as a French Cook is with Bacon, and each of them makes of his Performance a kind of Linsey-woolsey Composition.

As this Letter is grown too Bulky for the Post, it will come to your Hands by the Favour of a Gentleman, Major ——, who is to set out for London to-morrow Morning upon an Affair that requires his Expedition.

I can justly recommend him to your Acquaintance, as I have already referred him to yours; and I do assure you, that, by his ingenious and cheerful Conversation, he has not a little contributed, for a Twelvemonth past, to render my Exile more tolerable; it is true I might have sent the Sheets in Parcels, but I have chosen rather to surprise you with them all at once; and I dare say, bating Accidents, you will have the last of them sooner by his Means than by the ordinary Conveyance.